SOAR

A Psychotherapist's Journey from Heartache to Health

ANNIE WILLIAMS

Soar: A Psychotherapist's Journey from Heartbreak to Health

Content Warning- Note to Reader

This book is a personal journey told by the author that explores aspects of psychological and mental health issues. It includes abuse, loss, trauma, victimization, grief, suicidal thoughts/attempts, assaults, addiction, pregnancy loss/abortion, and violence. If you are a survivor of mental, physical, emotional abuse, or struggling with addiction, please utilize the resource page in the back of this book. Read with care and take breaks if feeling uneasy.

Dedication

I lovingly dedicate this book to my three beautiful children.
Written to provide a living history of their mother's life. You are and will always be the light of my life.

"The adventure in life is to learn. The purpose of life is to grow. The nature of life is to change. The challenge of life is to overcome. The essence of life is to care. The opportunity of life is to dare. The spice of life is to befriend. The beauty of life is to give." ~ **William Arthur Ward**

Thank you for all you have given me. ~ **Mom**

Table of Contents

Prologue

"The miracle is not that we do this work, but that we are happy to do it."
~Mother Teresa

Almost ten years into this endeavor, I still catch my breath when I walk into my private practice office. I set my purse down, turn on the lights and fire up my computer. I sink into my comfortable chair and review the upcoming clients for the day. I plan out and reflect on previous sessions and what the needs will be for the day.

I lean back in my chair, close my eyes, and begin to pray. "Thy Will be done, not mine. Let your words flow through me, and Lord, guide my tongue with compassion, wisdom, and Your word. Thank you for allowing me to do this work that I deeply love and respect." I wipe the tears from my eyes and take a few deep breaths before I call in my first client.

At times, Mental Health therapists talk amongst themselves about 'Imposter Syndrome.' This is when the therapist doubts their skills and has a persistent internalized fear of being exposed as a fraud. I have yet to meet a therapist that has not encountered this at some point in their career. For some, it is a daily occurrence, for others it is sporadic. I suppose the intensity of the emotional trauma our clients suffer from and reveal within sessions can have us doubt our capacity to assess, formulate a treatment plan, utilize the correct treatment modality, and execute the therapeutic session, all while being professional, compassionate, empathetic, ethical, and maintaining appropriate boundaries. All this is to be done while trying not to internalize the expressed trauma, but just enough to imagine what they must have felt on a visceral level. The phenomenon of internalizing these feelings too deeply can produce vicarious trauma, sometimes called compassion fatigue, for the therapist. This inevitably leads the therapist to feel exhaustion, anger, hypervigilance, irritability, isolation, anxiety, depression, and eventual total disruption of their own physical and/or mental health. This is often the reason therapists need their own therapist.

This persistent exposure to trauma experienced by others inevitably seeps into the heart of every therapist since it comes with the profession. Good self-care and boundaries are extremely important to the survival of a therapist. It is a constant push and pull for most. The desire to help and support as many clients in need as possible while respecting and understanding their own needs at the same time. For therapists raised in households that have poor or non-existent boundaries, this can be exceptionally difficult. I often wonder what percentage of therapists have been raised in an abusive household: mental, physical, sexual, and/or emotional abuse. I truly feel the number would be exceptionally high.

My desire to become a therapist began after spending years in therapy as a teen. I developed a deep appreciation for the benefits derived from talking and sharing your deepest, darkest fears and pain with someone impartial and professionally trained. The healing and growth that comes from that relationship is life- altering. It reminds me of a quote I read by an unknown author years ago.... *'Hurt people don't have to hurt people. Hurt people love people more. They become therapists, teachers, doctors, and social workers. Hurt people help people. Abusers are people who don't take responsibility for their lives and thus hurt people'*. I am a therapist who was hurt and took the steps to heal my trauma. The scars remain, and the memories still creep up to the surface, but I have tools to help manage the pain.

My purpose is to supply others with tools too. This is my story.

Chapter One

"Courage is fear that has said its prayers"
~ ***Dorothy Bernard***

He stood a good eight inches over everyone else on the school bus. That 4-miles-long drive from that modest two-story Midwestern home to John Wood Elementary School was a single, winding road, with the historic Dead Man's curve smack in the middle of the trip. My best friend, Trish Woods lived at the bottom of that deadly curve. Her parents had strategically planted Oak trees in their front yard, which would prohibit drunk drivers from flying from that curve into their living room window.

Victor Thompson was victorious in his ability to bully. He was picked up before me in the mornings and dropped off after me on the way home. He always wore those raggedy, plaid, bell-bottom pants with a wide-collared green shirt that was two sizes too small. Even at 10 years old, he stunk of underarm odor and the smell of wet dog. He ruled the bus, and every kid knew it, even the bus driver, Ms. Holland. Victor paced the isle between the rows of seats as the bus inched along, poking boys on the side of their heads as he passed, and leering at the girls, making intimidating gestures with his mouth. I always sat two rows from the back on the right-hand side, next to Trish. Even though she got on the bus after me, I made sure she sat next to the window. I watched Victor as he slinked his way towards the back of the bus. My head slightly tilted down, but my eyes never left his body. Trish would start to fiddle with her macramé purse and shift her body towards the window. His stink proceeded him and once it hit my nostrils, the adrenaline coursed throughout my body.

Today was the day. Momentarily, Victor would know I had reached my limit of silence and would feel the wrath of this 70-pound body. My hands trembled ever so slightly, but my will was strong. Victor slithered up beside me and reached his hand towards my hair. I placed my hands on the top of the seat in front of me to steady myself. I could almost hear Trish's heart beating within her chest cavity; or was that mine? Victor ran his tongue across his yellow, crooked teeth while he grabbed a lock of my hair. I grabbed his wrist and forced his arm away from me, which took a lock of hair with it. I leaped from my seat into the aisle and stood eye to collarbone with Victor, my archenemy. His bewilderment soon turned into a sadistic smile that spread ear to ear.

I soon felt a vice-like grip on my private parts that seemed so strong, it almost lifted me off the floor of the bus.

"What now Williams?" he seethed.

My fist clenched to punch him in the eye, but with further thought, I could not get a good enough swing as we were inches apart. I sunk my hand into his dirty blond hair and grabbed a fist full of greasy, long strands. I pulled with every ounce of might until he released my crotch and lost his balance, bringing him to the floor at my feet. Trish looked horrified and clenched her tattered purse against her chest.

I looked down on Victor as we pulled into the school bus loop and saw revenge deep in his hollow eyes. I knew retribution would be harsh and imminent. I stepped over him as I made my way towards the front of the bus, feeling the burn of the recent trauma to my private parts. Ms. Holland smacked her gum as she yelled for everyone to get off the bus, as the bell was about to ring. My legs trembled as I took those three big steps down the bus until I planted my feet firmly on the school grounds. I knew I would be safe from Victor at school, but I had to devise a plan for the trip home.

By an act of God, Victor was not there when school finished. Johnny Parker said his mom picked him up early from school as he had a stomachache and threw up on Jessica Gates. A wave of relief swept over my entire body as I sat down in my seat next to Trisha. She extended her slender hand towards mine, entwining our fingers as we remained quiet during the entire journey back to our house.

This was the best part of the day; coming home to Brutus, our middle-aged Alaskan Malamute that was a true sled dog and being outdoors until dusk. Spring was in full gear now; tulips were in bloom and daffodils reaching for the sky. There was a few lingering, small patches of snow around town, but those would melt by the end of the month. I threw my schoolbooks and lunch box into my bedroom, stripped out of my school clothes, put on my outside clothes, and threw myself on the ground to give Brutus the biggest hug I could give. His body wiggled all over with my hugs and his tail knocked my Mary Kay perfume bottle off my burrow. I giggled as we raced to see who would get down the stairs and to the front door first. The afternoon was filled with bike riding, tree climbing, somersaulting, and cloud watching. Brutus laid next to me as we lounged on our backs staring up at the sky and watching the clouds morph into animals, people, and ice cream cones. I would point and tell him what I saw, my dreams, my hopes, and my fears. He was my bestest of friends, my protector, my heart.

***

I was immensely proud of my banana seat, Schwinn bike. It had a basket in the front, but I refused to put on the handlebar streamers it came with, as that was a bit too girly for me. It was the end of the day, and I was losing steam; even Brutus looked tired. Rounding the bend to ride my bike into the garage, my foot slipped, and my private parts met the metal frame of the bicycle. The pain was quick and unrelenting. I was still very tender from Victor's wrath, but this was like pouring salt into a wound. I walked gingerly into the house, and my mother, standing at the stove cooking dinner was instantly aware of my gait. My mother inquired about the incident, so I fabricated a false story to conceal the truth which I often did with her. I did not want the usual onslaught of questions where answers never led to her satisfaction.

She would not let it go. I told her I hurt my leg riding my bike, but it would be fine in a few minutes. She insisted I strip down in the kitchen for her to examine my body. I removed my pants and stood there with tears starting to well up in my eyes. I just wanted to go to my room, lay on the floor with Brutus, and listen to my record player.

She scanned my legs and barked, "Remove your underwear."

I begged her that it was not necessary, but her patience ran thin as she yanked down my panties. I stood frozen in the kitchen, ground beef burning in the frying pan, while my mother looked me over. She gasped as she saw the large, swollen, purple bruise on my pubic bone. She demanded to know where I got this.

"Don't lie. You slipping off your bike did not do this."

It all came flooding out; Victor, the bus, my rage, his hands on me. She told me to get dressed and go to my room. All the while, she cursed me for ruining dinner since it was now burnt.

"All you do is lie, Annie. You are just a pathetic liar."

I ran up the stairs, shut my door, threw myself on my bed, and cried into my pile of blankets. I sobbed as quietly as possible, so I could hear her footsteps on the stairs if she were coming to my room. I heard a sniffing at the door and realized Brutus wanted to come in. I eased the door open just enough for him to squeeze through and closed it quickly but quietly behind him. I pulled two blankets from my bed onto the floor: one for me and one for Brutus. We laid there, nose-to-nose, on my bedroom floor praying for tomorrow afternoon to come quickly.

The next morning, my mother waited with me at the end of our long driveway for my bus to arrive. This was not normal, but she promised me she just wanted to say 'hi' to Ms. Holland and would then be on her way back into the house; with this, my anxiety dissipated. A few minutes passed until you could hear the low rumble of the bus engine chugging around the bend.

My mother came from an upper-class family that resided in a sprawling mansion in the Catskills of New York. She was raised by maids and butlers since her parents were preoccupied with entertaining their numerous nearest and dearest friends frequently. Per my mother, her mother was a raging alcoholic who liked to belittle and degrade her. At the age of 12 years old, my mother was dropped off at a boarding school, and "left to rot" there. My mother watched her school years tick by with other student's parents visiting on spring break and holidays, while she sat alone in her dorm room, waiting for parents that would never show.

She eventually married, had three children, divorced, married again, and had me. She often told me the only reason I was conceived was to make my father love her more and to stop screwing around on her. That statement was always followed by her extreme disappointment that those plans never came to fruition.

"The only time he would screw me is if the moon and stars were in the correct alignment, and he had enough beers under his belt."

Hearing this made my stomach turn. She became the first female police officer in our small town of Chester. She frequently said to me, "It's a man's world out there, Annie. You have to be tough to survive." She eventually left her profession after a robber she put in jail was released and later broke into our home in the middle of the night. He brutally raped her as we kids slept upstairs, and he left her for dead wrapped around the back of a toilet in our basement laundry area.

The bus pulled up to the end of the driveway, and my mother stepped onto the bus. Ms. Holland looked bewildered and asked, "Why are you getting on the bus?"

My mother asked, "Who is Victor?" My heart sank deep into my chest as I felt the blood run from my face.

"Ms. Meedle, you cannot come onto the bus," said Ms. Holland.

"Ms. Holland, you know I am a police officer, and I can get on any Godforsaken bus I damn well please. So... I ask you again, who is Victor?"

Ms. Holland reluctantly pointed to Victor who was now sitting in my seat, two rows from the back, and stated, "There he is."

My mother began to walk down the aisle of the bus towards Victor. With each row she passed, her fingernails scratched the tops of the plastic school bus seats. The silence was deafening, except for Ms. Holland continuing to state, "Ms. Meedle, please get off the bus. I will get in trouble."

I stood next to Ms. Holland while she sat in the driver's seat, watching as if life turned into slow motion. My mother stopped in front of Victor, and asked, "Are you Victor?"

He sheepishly mumbled, "Yes."

"Stand up, Victor." He slowly looked side to side as if the reason he was to stand would be written on the grungy school bus windows.

"Be a man and stand up from your seat," her voice more insistent.

Victor stumbled to his feet and met my mother eye-to-eye.

My mother firmly wrapped her hand around Victor's crotch and clamped down hard. Victor squealed in pain. His legs and arms began to tremble. Ms. Holland, now with radio in hand, insisted in a fevered pitch that my mother exit the bus immediately.

My mother, looking like a rabid dog seething, "You touch my daughter again, I will rip off your baby penis and balls, then shove them down your disgusting, foul mouth. Do we understand each other"?

Victor had tears streaming down his red cheeks and screamed out, "Yes! Yes! Please let me go!" My mother eventually released her vice and slowly turned around to head back down the aisle of the bus. Victor scrambled and then collapsed into his regular seat. Ms. Holland was in utter dismay, as the gum in her gaping mouth almost fell out and onto the floor.

"Have a lovely day Ms. Holland," my mother said as she exited the bus. My mother stood at the end of the drive, fists clenched, and spun slowly around scanning the outside bus windows until her eyes met mine. Her look was cold and heartless, while one corner of her mouth turned up into a smile. She walked towards the house as I willed my lead feet to find my seat on the bus.

My parents divorced when I was two years old. The only memory I have of my dad living in our home was him and I sitting crisscross on the kitchen floor with two bowls of ice cream. We giggled as we each took a spoonful from each other's dish. He left. I do not remember the day, but little did I know at the time, it left a hole in my heart. I had three older stepsiblings who lived in the home with me, two sisters and one brother. Sandy was fifteen, Jeffery was thirteen, and Louise was nine when I was born. When out in public, people would often mistake my sister Sandy for my mother as she was six feet tall and looked older than fifteen. I remember her as gentle, kind, nurturing, and a mother figure. She had long, soft, brown hair that tickled my cheek when she held me on her hip. She left. I do not remember the day, but that was the day I lost the loving buffer between me and my mother. Mom said Sandy ran away from home 17 years ago, and for months my mother thought she was dead. She said police found her wallet floating in the Chicago River, but mother's borderline personality frequently led to dramatic fabrications. I was told Sandy got lost in the seventy's haze of drugs and free love, and with that, another loss.

My brother and I would spend hours lying on his bedroom floor listening to The Who, Pink Floyd, and The Rolling Stones on his record player. He became my father figure after dad left, and I loved him dearly. He frequently had a lost look in his eye as if he were asking the Heavens for an answer. An answer to what I do not know. Jeffrey ran away a year later after turning down a full ride scholarship for swimming to any college of his choice. I do not remember the day he left, but that was the day I lost my father figure. This left me and my sister, Louise in the home with my mother and her numerous boyfriends and lovers that frequented our home daily.

Some boyfriends took an interest in my sister and I, and some would see us as obstacles to my mother's freedom. Many were fellow police officers who would furnish our meager home with stolen items they would take after busting home burglars. This delighted my mother, and she would repay them with free reign to her body.

One of them took a special interest in me. George Weber was a dirty cop through and through. He was married, like most of them were, and would glare at me from the corner of his eye. He would occasionally scan my body and lick his lips until his eyes met mine. I took every measure to escape his gaze and his presence whenever possible.

On a beautiful Sunday morning, I was getting ready to be picked up by my father for our weekly day together. My mother called me over to a hallway mirror and handed me a piece of paper. There was a nervous energy about her as she gripped my shoulders. She told me to recite the words aloud on the page while facing the mirror, as her and George would listen. I began reading her handwritten words. "I do not want to live with my father. He makes me have sex with him. He hurts me and touches me in certain places."

I looked in the mirror, my mother and George flanking me on either side and stated, "This is not true. He doesn't do any of these things to me." My mother prompted me to keep reading and that it will be memorized by the end of the day. I begged her to not do this and that I did not want to say these lies.

She stated, "You will say these things when we go to court with your father. You will look him in the eye while you are on the stand and say these words for the judge and God to hear."

Still standing at the mirror with them behind me, tears streaming down my face, I pleaded with her. She said, "George, show Annie what will happen if she does not follow through with this in court."

George slowly removed his firearm from his holster and brought it up to my temple. He pulled back the trigger as I closed my eyes tightly. They both burst out laughing as urine streamed down my leg onto the floor. George holstered his gun and tossed me a towel to clean up the mess I made on the floor.

"You are so pathetic, Annie. You're good at lying, this should be a walk in the park for you."

Soon thereafter, I took my regular spot at the top of the tree in our front yard, waiting to see my dad's red Oldsmobile with a white top come around Dead Man's curve. I would make it to the bottom of the tree before he pulled into the driveway. I slid into the red leather passenger seat, closed the door, and began to sob. I then looked up at the front window of my home and saw my mother and George peering out the window with disapproving looks on their faces. I told my father to drive, but he insisted I explain why I was upset before he would leave the driveway. I begged him to just get me out of there, but he held firm to me explaining first. It all came spilling out of me. As I choked out the words, I knew I would receive retaliation from my mother for telling. I was gasping for air as the words fell out of my mouth.

My eyes met his when I was finished speaking, and the utter hatred he had for my mother was clear on his face. "Son of a bitch. I will kill her."

He reached for the car door handle as I grabbed his arm, so he would not leave the car and confront my mother and George. I begged and pleaded for him not to go to the front door and screamed, "They will kill me if you do!"

With this, he paused mid-step of exiting the car and plopped back down into the driver's seat. He clutched the steering wheel with both hands, knuckles turning white.

He looked over at me with tears in his eyes and said, "We will not go to court. You do not have to say those things ever. I will stop fighting and you can stay here."

A wave of bittersweet relief came over me, but sorrow quickly followed. I had to go home to my mother this evening after our visit, and my father was giving up on me. Another loss. I was going to be stuck in that home forever. As we backed out of the driveway, my plan became clear—survive, then run once I was old enough to care for myself.

I opened the door to my home that evening and quietly slinked into the house. My mother was standing at the end of the hallway with her arms crossed as if she never left that spot in front of the mirror.

She said, "Welcome home, Annie. How was your visit with your father"?

I knew whatever answer I gave would be the wrong answer, so I stayed silent. My eyes shifted to Brutus sitting motionless in the middle of the living room. He knew what was about to come.

"Come into my room, Annie. I have something for you," she said.

Tears began to stream down my face, and I begged her to let me go to my room. She ushered me into her room, and as all the times before, calmly said, "remove all your clothes."

I pleaded with her, but her tone escalated with every plea. "Annie, this always hurts me more than you, but you leave me no choice."

I removed all my clothing and assumed the regular position leaning over her bed. Her bedroom walls were covered in mirrors, and I watched as she stood behind me and removed her police belt with the buckle of the police department on it. She raised it into the air as far as her arm could reach and began to whip me. She rarely whipped my bottom, only the back of my thighs and lower back. I watched as she continued to throw her arm up into the air with the belt and then made contact with my body.

"I only do this because I love you Annie," she mumbled. Her smile would grow larger with each round, she would stop once all her rage and anger depleted from her soul.

I was dismissed to my room where I examined my wounds in the full-length mirror on my closet door. I counted the number of swollen strips across my legs and lower back to see if it was more or less than the last beating. Sometimes it was hard to tell, as many stripes were still evident from the last encounter. *Why does love have to hurt so badly?* I thought. Redressing was a painful task, but the clothes masked the marks on my skin.

Eventually, I hear the sniffing at my bedroom door. I quietly let Brutus into my bedroom, and we laid on my bed as he licked the salty tears from my cheeks. "I love you Brutus. More than you will ever know."

I was content with missing dinner that night and drifting to sleep. On the verge of slumber, I heard footsteps climbing the stairs. They were not the footsteps of my sister Louise but of my mother. I wrapped my arms tighter around Brutus' neck and held my breath. The door swung open, and I could only see my mother's shadow against the hallway light behind her. She was holding something in her right hand I could not make out until she crossed the threshold into my room.

She barked, "Get up, you have not completed your chores for the day."

I jumped out of bed, and she tossed me the bucket full of cleaning supplies she was holding. A sense of relief came over me, as this may please my mother.

She stated, "You are going to do things a little different this time." She handed me the vacuum and said, "Since you did not complete your chores during the daytime, you have lost the luxury of using lights while you clean." She shoved me down the basement stairs and said, "Get to work."

I was terrified of the basement. It was dark, damp and smelled musty. The basement was partially finished with carpet, couches, and a pool table. The other half was unfinished with cement floors, a large laundry area, a creepy closet with a red door, and a bathroom. I do not know why, but I never ventured into that dark closet. It was a space I could see myself getting trapped in and getting swallowed whole.

I vacuumed the basement carpet and stairs in pitch dark. My heart was beating so fiercely in my ears, I could barely hear the vacuum running. Tears streamed down my eyes as I prayed I would finish before a monster crept up behind me and ate me alive. Minutes felt like hours down in that loud darkness.

Once done, I ran up the stairs and threw open the door to the kitchen. "There is no way you are done down there", my mother bellowed. "If I go check what you've done and it's not clean, you will spend the rest of the night in the basement."

She remained sitting at the kitchen table, thank God, and had my next chore ready to go. I saw a toothbrush, cleaning powder, and bucket of water sitting in the middle of the kitchen. She barked, "Take off your pants and get on your knees. I want you to feel the hard floor against your kneecaps as you scrub the floor from one end to the other."

That night I spent hours on my hands and knees, toothbrush in hand, scrubbing the floor. I was grateful to be in the well-lit kitchen versus the dark basement. Brutus sat at the entryway to the kitchen, head laying in his outstretched arms, watching my every move. I imagined him cheering me on, urging me to finish so we could crawl into bed. It felt like my kneecaps were bruised and swollen. My fingertips were worn down with the use of scrubbing powder grinding between my hand and the toothbrush. I finished the floor and was finally allowed to go to bed. I think she was tired of monitoring me and wanted to go to bed herself. Back to my safe place with my best friend.

Chapter Two

"I'm not a product of my circumstances. I am a product of my decisions"
~ ***Stephen Covey***

On warm summer nights, we slept with the windows open. If the wind was blowing in the right direction, I could hear the southbound train from Chicago making its way to Michigan City. The faint sound of its whistle when it crossed a busy road was a beautiful sound. I imagined the people on the train, full of wonderment and hope as they chugged along towards their destination. If I listened very closely, I could hear the wheels clicking on the rails of the track. 'Click-click, click-click.'

Were the people looking out the train window also watch trees and houses fly by like I did while traveling in the car? Did they have the same thoughts I did? Wanting and aching to be somewhere different? Were they allowed to bring a real dog or only stuffed dogs on the train with them? All questions I would need to find out before my time to escape.

Summer was ending like a sweet dream and the evenings were becoming crisp and cool. I spent every possible moment outside, playing in the yard, picking dandelions for Ralphie, my grey and white stuffed dog, and gathering apples from the uppermost branches of the apple tree. My mother would make the most delicious apple pies and tarts. About once a month, my mother and I would gather all the garden snakes and place them in the garden against the back wall of our house. The snakes would eat the spiders in the garden and prevent them from entering the house when the weather became cool. We each put on long pants and gloves and would go on a snake hunt. It felt so comforting to be working in tandem with my mother. On these rare occasions, I felt so much love for her.

When we found a long, black Racer, we quickly grabbed it by the tail and swung it like a pendulum to prevent it from biting our legs or arms. They of course were not poisonous, but their bite with needle-sharp teeth would be enough to leave a nasty bruise and small puncture wound. The fear and excitement of catching the snakes was exhilarating. Once we got close to them, they would raise their head and pose to strike. The trick was to get behind them and pluck them up by the tail as quickly as possible before they could get in the first strike. If the grab was off and it landed in the middle of the snake, it was much more difficult to avoid the bite. We would usually find 15-20 each search which was sufficient for our garden. The more in the garden and not the yard was ideal for me, as cartwheels and somersaults leading to an unexpected encounter with a snake was not a pleasant experience.

Fall turned to winter and the days grew shorter. On one bitterly cold but sunny day after school, Brutus and I geared up for tobogganing. Adorning my heavy snowsuit, mittens, hat and boots, Brutus and I headed to the garage for the beautiful, wooden toboggan. He was dancing with anticipation, spinning, and jumping in circles. We placed the toboggan at the end of the driveway overlooking the acre property where we resided. The one-acre backyard seemed to go for miles and miles. Not a house in sight past our property line. The property had a steep slope from the edge of the driveway and leveled out a half-acre down. With a toboggan, Brutus and I could reach a high enough speed to make it to the frozen pond at the end of our yard.

I climbed aboard the toboggan, Brutus standing at my side. "You ready Brutus?" as he yelped in excitement.

I put my hands on either side of the toboggan and shimmied back and forth gathering steam to push off and make it across the frozen pond. With one last burst of energy, I took hold of the reigns, then we descended the hill at a rapid pace. Snow sprayed up over the front of our toboggan and stung my face as we flew down. Brutus ran alongside and kept pace with me, as I wiped the snow off my eyelashes. The push was good enough to hit the pond and slide across to the other side. I jumped off, and rough housed in the snow with Brutus. He was so proud of our accomplishment and now was his time to shine.

I hooked the reign on the toboggan to the collar around his neck. Brutus could hardly contain his excitement and wanted to take off before I could get seated. I finally climbed into the toboggan and gave Brutus the word, "Go!"

He shot off so quickly, I almost fell backwards and out the back of the toboggan. I righted myself and held on for dear life. He dragged me up the hill with the determination of a full team of sled dogs. And once we reached the peak, it would be difficult for him to remember when to stop. Maybe he did not want the excitement to end. We eventually came to a halt one hundred feet into the driveway. I unhooked his collar and praised him for a job well done. He returned the compliment by licking the snowflakes off my cheeks and nose. After a few more runs, it was becoming dusk, and the moon started to rise. The snowflakes glistened in its light, and the trees looked like they were adorned with twinkling lights as they swayed in the gentle wind.

My mother was in a good mood that evening because one of her boyfriends was over at the house. I looked forward to their visits, as it diverted her attention from me. I was free to be myself and enjoy time with Brutus. We gathered at the dinner table, my sister, mother, her boyfriend, and myself. We always had fruit cocktails served with dinner. Without fail, I would save this for last as a wonderful way to finish off my meal. That night, there were peas on our plates, and I hated peas. I ate everything but the peas and got ready to enjoy my fruit cocktail. I scooped a heaping spoonful into my mouth and spat it into my napkin. It tasted like a gallon of salt was dumped into my serving. My sister giggled and pointed to the saltshaker on the table. Every time she did this, I vowed to myself I would keep an eye on my plate and catch her the next time, but never did. I pouted, looking at the mound of peas still sitting on my plate next to the salted fruit cocktail.

My mother cleared the table and everyone but me stood up and left for the living room. "Annie, you are not dismissed until you clear your plate."

There was no arguing this demand, as I knew the outcome. I sat there staring at the peas while minutes turned to hours and hours turned to bedtime. I refused to eat those damn peas and that ruined fruit cocktail. The kitchen lights were turned off and all headed to bed as I sat there, head rested on my arm. I would eventually give into sleep, until jostled awake to go to bed. My sister's actions filled me with resentment and anger. She constantly bullied me and took pleasure in playing cruel jokes on me.

***

One of my earliest memories is toting around Ralphie by his grey and white arm. He was my favorite companion, after Brutus of course. Ralphie, a stuffed curly haired, floppy-eared dog was usually adorned in a red and white polka-dotted dress meant for my baby doll. He was soft, squishy, and loved on to the point of tattered ears, scuffed-up glass eyes and crooked black nose. He took part in almost all the adventures Brutus, and I went on. Ralphie especially liked when I picked him a bouquet of dandelions from the backyard and held it up to his nose to get a big whiff of springtime.

On a cool morning, Brutus, Ralphie and I prepared for our regular Saturday hike. We packed only the essentials for survival... a compass, a Swiss army pocketknife, a bologna sandwich, two extra slices of bread, a safety pin, one piece of thin string, and a medium silver thermos filled with well water. Our supplies were carefully placed in a white pillowcase with little blue flowers on it, and once completed, the opening was tied in a knot. I then tied each end of a small rope to the knot and placed the homemade purse across my chest. I hurried into my hiking outfit which I carefully laid out the evening before... long pants, tall boots to protect myself from snake bits, a plaid long-sleeved flannel shirt for protection against prickers, a light blue windbreaker for warmth and a red checkered handkerchief wrapped around my head and tied as the nape of my neck. Ralphie had his own yellow checkered handkerchief he wore in the same fashion.

Brutus could barely hold back his excitement as I opened the back door. We bounded down the damp wooden steps past the garden to the crest of the hill. We stood in awe, as we did every weekend, at the vast land in front of us. The yard gracefully descended until plateauing off midway down. At the base of the hill stood a badminton net. Tall, thick brush lined the end of the property which seemed to extend for miles. A handful of tall oak and weeping willow trees stood like protectors over the thick brush. A couple of oaks had strategically place hunter's stands perched high up into its branches. I knew every square inch of that land, from every quicksand pit to every wild berry patch. Brutus lifted his snout and drew in a breath of springtime air deep into his lungs; I followed suit. With that, we were off. Inevitably, my feet could not keep up with my forward motion down the hill and I would end up cartwheeling down until reaching the base. I laughed at the predictability of my tumble as Brutus danced circles around me, waiting for me to find my feet again.

Things always became serious once we entered the brush, as we had to keep watch for snakes, white-tailed deers, banana spiders (also known as the Black and Yellow Garden Spider), stray dogs and orange outfitted hunters. We periodically would come upon a clearing where we sat and drank some water. I would pour a thermos cup full for Brutus first, then one for myself and Ralphie. We sat in the grass and let ladybugs crawl up our legs until they took off flying. One landed on Brutus's nose which made him crossed-eyed as he tried to focus on it. I burst out laughing sending Brutus into a happy dance. After our break, we pushed onward to the biggest oak with the highest tree stand. Brutus did not care for this much as he would have to wait at the base of the tree as Ralphie and I climbed up to the stand. Brutus would settle down at the base of the tree in a bed of corn left out by hunters. Once in the stand, Ralphie and I shared our quickly made bologna sandwich. I tore off small pieces of bread and dropped them down to Brutus. He caught them gracefully as if they were snowflakes falling from the Heavens.

We luckily never encountered a hunter while in his stand. I was always on alert for this and felt Brutus and my trusty pocketknife would protect us if an encounter turned physical. The view was breathtaking. The top of the Oaks shimmered in the high- noon sunlight. Little acorns fell as the wind whispered through its branches. In nature with senses heightened, I imagined the sound of falling acorns hitting the ground below could be heard miles away. Occasionally, poor Brutus caught one on the top of his head. The birds would soon be gorging on the ripe fruit of the Black Cherry tree that stood tall by the thicket of blackberry bushes. Ralphie and I laid back on the wooden floorboards of the tree stand and gazed up at the light blue sky peeking out through the swaying tree branches. I wanted to stay here, just like this forever. The gentle breeze caressed the hair off my brow and the sunshine healed my soul. I dreamed of days filled with consistent love, understanding, and lasting acceptance. I squeezed Ralphie close to my chest as tears fell from my eyes onto my handkerchief. I knew one day I would soar like the hawks overhead, but for now, freedom was found in that deer stand.

The compass was rarely used as we tracked our direction by the sun's position in the sky. Once it hit about 2 o'clock, we knew it was time to turn around and head home. We had one more stop at Sugar Creek on the way back. Sugar Creek was a narrow, winding stream that cut through the thick brush. The land from the edge of the stream and out by five feet was dirt, stones, acorns, leaves and an occasional arrowhead. The branches of a couple tall Oaks canopied the creek and occasionally dropped its acorns into the shallow, swift flowing stream. Brutus found his regular spot in between the large, exposed roots of his favorite tree. I opened the knot to our supplies and pulled out the safety pin, thin string, and extra slices of bread. I searched for the perfect stick; one not too big, but not too small. It had to be fairly straight and lively as dead branches would break too easily. After searching, with the perfect stick in hand, I assembled my fishing rod. I tore off a small piece of bread and wet it in the stream to make a small, doughy ball. I put the dough on the open end of the safety pin and dropped it into the flowing water. The dough would only last a minute or two before it disintegrated off the safety pin. I carefully rationed the bread to get the most uses as possible. I dropped a fresh dough ball squeezed onto the hook into the water.

Finally, a tugging on the line. I was so excited; I pulled hard on the stick and out came a rainbow trout attached to my makeshift pole. Mid yank, the trout flew off the hook and landed at Brutus's feet. The tiny fish flopped around getting covered with dead leaves and dirt. Brutus flung himself out of his tree root bed and starred sheepishly at the floundering trout. I was so excited with my catch that I tripped running to retrieve my prize and dove face-first into the dirt, landing eye to eye with the exasperated fish. Brutus looked at both of us trying to make sense of the debacle. I gently picked it up and rushed to the water's edge to clean it off. I let the water flow over it to wash away the leaves and dirt. As I held it in the water, no bigger than the length of my 10-year-old hand, I wondered if it was big enough for a fish fry tonight. If not, how many more would I need to catch?

In the sunshine, the scales shimmered the colors of the rainbow. I knew I would have to decide soon as to keep or release it. A few feet upstream, I saw a couple of other small trout swimming against the current as if suspended in time, seemingly waiting on my decision as well. Maybe one of them was its mom or dad wanting their son back. My mind then flashed to making my mother happy that I would supply dinner tonight. Maybe she would even love me more? Maybe I would be free from a beating tonight if I brought home fish for dinner? After what felt like an eternity for me, I decided to let it go. I watched it aggressively swim upstream until out of sight.

I sat at the edge of the water, Brutus sitting by my side, and I threw my arm around him and drew him closer. "Well, best buddy, no fish for dinner tonight." We enjoyed the last slice of white bread as we stared at our satisfied reflection in the water.

We made it home right before the crickets started their routine chirping. The sun was drawing close to the horizon and the birds seemed to be settling down for the evening. We sat on the grass by the edge of the garden reflecting on the day's adventure. It was time to go inside for dinner, and with some luck, it would be uneventful. My mother seemed to be in a good mood that evening, so I anticipated a boyfriend would be arriving shortly. A large, empty mason jar sat next to the stove, close to where my mother was browning ground beef for dinner. I sat in the kitchen starring out the window as the day closed and night took over. The mini flashes of light increased by the minute as the lightning bugs came out to play.

"Mom! I need that mason jar to catch lightning bugs, so I can take them to my room at bedtime!" My mother happily agreed, punched some holes into the lid for air, and told me to hurry before dinner was ready. I grabbed the jar and Brutus beat me to the back door. I grabbed the butterfly net on the way out to the backyard.

It is amazing how different everything looks at night to a child. The grass was soft and cool on my bare feet as I ran through the yard holding the butterfly net above my head. The only light I could see was the soft glow of the kitchen light, the millions of pinpoint lights in the night sky and the occasional glow from the dozens of lightning bugs. After Brutus and I were satisfied with the ten or so lightning bugs floating in the mason jar, we headed inside. I couldn't wait to finish dinner so I could go to bed and experience my own personal light display.

I laid in bed, Ralphie tucked under my arm and stared at the magical light display taking place on my bedside table. I wondered where the lightning bugs went during the day. What did they eat? Did they have brothers and sisters? My eyes grew heavy with questions I did not have answers to. The following day, my previous amazement turned into fear. The fireflies that had been inside the mason jar were now lifeless at the bottom. The guilt coursed through my entire body like adrenaline. My mother came into my room to wake me for the day and saw the tears in my eyes. She asked me why I was crying, and I said that the lightning bugs died. I knew looking for sympathy from my mother was like rolling the dice on a craps table. Sometimes the response was loving and nurturing, but most often it was the opposite.

"Annie, what did you expect? Of course, they are dead! You are such a stupid, hateful little girl. You probably knew they would die when you put them in that jar. I'm surprised Brutus is still alive after you tried to kill him by sitting on him."

My mother would never miss an opportunity to guilt me about the time I was 5 years old and tried to ride on Brutus like a horse. Brutus yelped when I did this, and my mother flew off the couch, grabbed me, plucked me off Brutus, and threw me hard onto the floor. Brutus gnashed his teeth at my mother for her rough behavior, and he was punished for this by being kicked hard in the stomach. The guilt I felt for unintentionally hurting Brutus lived in my heart like a lead weight.

She screamed, "Get up, throw away the bugs, and clean out the jar." I scrambled out of bed and grabbed the jar.

I did not make further eye contact with her, as I learned that was a direct challenge which usually resulted in the belt. I passed her, clutching the mason jar, at the threshold of my bedroom doorway. I stood at the top of the stairs, getting ready to go down to the kitchen when she grabbed a fistful of my hair on the back of my head.

She bent over to place her mouth against my ear. "Did you say something?" she seethed.

Tears started to stream down my face and onto my nightgown, "No, mom."

She hissed, "Yes, you did. You know what happens when you talk back to me."

With that, she shoved my head forward while releasing the fistful of hair. I went headfirst down the flight of shag-green carpeted stairs. The mason jar practically exploded between my body and the stairs in the fall. I landed at the bottom with dead lightning bugs smashed into my pink nightgown. The breath was knocked out of me when I landed on my back at the base of the stairs. I laid there gasping for air, scratching at my neck trying to get air into my shaking body. Air finally filled my lungs when she descended the stairs towards me. A sinister smile came over her face halfway down as each foot sternly landed on each stair.

She stepped over my body, dropped to her knees, leaned into place her mouth against my ear and whispered, "Clean this shit up."

Still laying at the bottom of the stairs on the wooden floor, I looked over into the living room where Brutus lay on the floor in the sunlight streaming through the window. His eyes met mine and I knew I was loved by someone.

***

Liz, my other bestest friend lived the next small town over from me. We went to the same school as there were many small towns with one elementary school system. We spent at least one to two Saturdays a month together which always turned into a sleepover. Her family lived on a small farm that housed chickens, horses, and pigs. Her neighbor, Mr. Pots, was the grumpy old man that lived next door to the right of Liz's home. Mr. Willard lived to the left of her house but was rarely home as he worked in the city. Mr. Pots did not have a working farm, but he had patches of corn, wild berry bushes and a watermelon patch. Those berries were like pieces of candy hanging from tiny twigs just waiting to be picked and gobbled up. His watermelons were small in size, but sweeter than any farmer's market I had ever been to.

Mr. Pots' watermelon patch was in the southeast corner of his acreage, furthest away from Liz's property line. Liz has a small wooden, single-story barn at the center back of her yard. There were thigh-high Switchgrass that started from the side of Liz's barn, stretching across the back end of Mr. Pots' property until reaching his watermelon patch. He spent many hours working his land, tilling the ground, feeding his animals and watering his garden. Liz and I, peering out the large door, waited patiently in the barn, with a knife in hand for him to retire back into his home. We plotted out our devious plan on how we would reach his watermelon patch, take one watermelon, and make it back to the barn without being detected.

We whispered in hushed tones, so our presence would not be detected despite Mr. Pots being a good acre away from our covert location.

"We need to crawl on our bellies," I explained, "he caught us last time when we were just running hunched over."

Liz exclaimed, "I know that! I was there last time, remember?" We broke out in a nervous, hushed laughter.

“Okay, don’t forget to look out for snakes and banana spiders,” Liz prompted.

“I think we should crawl one in front of the other and not side by side, so we don’t crush more grass than we need too,” I decided.

“We will leave the knife and our jackets here in the barn,” Liz said.

We surely did not want our bright red and orange jackets to be on our bodies during our mission, flashing like a beacon for Mr. Pots’ attention. He warned us last time he caught us red-handed, on our knees in his garden, dirt-covered watermelon in hand that he would tell Liz’s parents. With pleading eyes, we gazed up at Mr. Pots and swore on all that was holy that we would never lay foot on his property again.

After what seemed like an eternity, Mr. Pots finally finished his chores and headed back to the house. With mouths salivating, we assumed the position on our bellies and army crawled through the thick grasses. Liz, knowing the property best, went first while I followed closely behind at her feet. The grass crunched loud enough to wake the dead as we crushed it under our body weight. We stopped every few feet to listen in silence for Mr. Pots’ footsteps. Every twenty feet or so, Liz would immediately halt her crawl and let out a sharp whimper. It would either be a sharp rock scraping across her belly or coming face-to-face with a large banana spider perched in the center of her enormous web.

Finally, we made it to the clearing at the edge of the watermelon patch. This is when we were most vulnerable, as we were now in clear view of Mr. Pots’ kitchen window. While our bodies were still in the cover of the brush, with only our heads poking out, we scanned the patch looking for the closest watermelon. Once located, we conversed, debated, and agreed on our target. Only one person would leave the safety of the brush to grab the watermelon, since it would create less possibility of our movement catching Mr. Pots’ attention. Liz went last time, so it was my turn.

My heart pounded hard in my chest and my hands started to tremble. There was no turning back now; we were committed. I decided to keep with the army crawl as it would be less noticeable than running hunched over. The only problem was crawling took more time to complete the mission, and longer visibility. Once clearing the brush, I felt so vulnerable, as if I were crawling naked for the entire world to see. I reached the watermelon, plucked it from its resting place off the vine and realized I could not crawl and carry it at the same time.

I suddenly felt paralyzed. "Now what?" I whispered to myself. I heard Liz's irritated whisper, "Come on! Move now!"

Panic set in and I could just feel Mr. Pots' eyes laser-focused on me from his window. I tucked the volleyball sized melon under my arm, found my trembling feet, and took off like a lightning bolt towards Liz. Once hitting the grass, I stayed on my feet, hunched over, and ran as fast as possibly towards the barn. I did not care about banana spiders or the snakes. I did not care I left Liz in the grasses. I did not care about anything but getting to that barn undetected.

Liz was so panicked I left her behind she took off running as well. We both dove into the barn, landing in a pile of hay and pig manure. I flipped to my back in mid-flight, so I would not land on top of the watermelon and smash it under my weight. We both laid there, in pig poop, in silence waiting to hear Mr. Pots screaming for us. Nothing.

"We made it! We made it!" Liz exalted. We grabbed clumps of hay to wipe the poop from my back and Liz's breastbone.

I grabbed the knife, my hand still trembling in fear and cut into the ripe, dirty watermelon. I cut it into quarters, and with juice streaming down our forearms, we devoured the red, juicy innards, seeds, and all. A guttural 'ummm' came from both of us as we finished our feast right down to the rind. We were sufficiently filled as we put our jackets back on over our still-wet, sticky arms and headed back up to the house. Thoroughly satisfied with our mission, we entered Liz's house through the front door and ran smack into the backside of Mr. Pots standing in the living room talking to Liz's mom. We couldn't have appeared more guilty even if we actively tried. Our eyes were wide and panicked, I still clutched the knife with pink watermelon juice oozing off it, and our mouths were still wet and sticky from the fruit.

It was already determined by Liz's mom and Mr. Pot what our punishment would be before Liz and I even hit the front doorsteps.

"Liz and Annie," Mr. Pots calmly stated, "since you love my watermelon patch as much as I do, you will spend three Saturdays over the summer helping me harvest my crops."

I would have agreed to spend the next 20 summers helping him if they agreed not to tell my mother of this incident. Tears flowed down my face, and I pleaded with Mr. Pots and Liz's mother, "Please do not tell my mother about this. I will do anything you ask me to." Mr. Pots and Liz's mother looked at each other and agreed to keep this amongst the four of us. I was fairly certain they knew my mother's temperament and were not interested in involving her.

I learned a lot about planting and harvesting that summer from Mr. Pots. Liz and I worked hard on his property clearing land, sowing seeds, and gathering fruits and vegetables once ready. On our last day, covered head-to-toe in dirt, we saw a side of Mr. Pots we never saw before. His eyes softened, and he thanked us for our help.

He stated, "Now go pick out one watermelon for each of you and we can enjoy them on the back stoop." We giggled and followed his orders. We picked the two biggest, ripest melons and brought them to the garden hose to rinse off. Once done, we gathered around Mr. Pots stoop as evening approached. We sat crossed legged on the concrete and ate until our stomachs almost burst. The sun set on a long day as the lightning bugs came out to play.

"Now, it's time to get home," Mr. Pots said as he helped us gather up the left-over rinds. "You both are welcome on my land at any time but enter it through my front door."

We shook sticky hands on it and started for Liz's home. I stopped momentarily and looked back at Mr. Pots as he stood on his back stoop watching us head home. I thought I saw a tear in his eye, but I could not quite tell. I waved good-bye and we kept on our way. Two weeks later, Liz's mom received word that Mr. Pots died peacefully in his bed in the middle of the night. We did not know at that time what a wonderful gift he gave us. A lesson of love, compassion and strength that would never be forgotten.

Chapter Three

"Out of the mountain of despair, a stone of hope."
~ *Martin Luther King Jr.*

Three months later, I was anxiously waiting on the green velvet couch for my birthday guests to arrive. The clock ticked in the eerily quiet living room so loudly that it kept pace with my heartbeat. I kept running to the window overlooking the driveway when I heard a car approaching. My mother painstakingly sewed a ballerina costume for me which seemed to take her months to create. She frequently made all my Halloween and birthday-themed costumes. The tutu was beautiful with multicolored sparkles throughout the layers of tulle and the shoes had the same sparkles covering them. She curled and pinned up my hair to accent the crown on top of my head.

My birthday was days before Halloween, so every year I was allowed a huge costume party with a minimum of twelve girlfriends. The parties were always filled with fun and laughter which spilled over to the next day, as there was always a sleepover. The house was adorned with spooky Halloween decorations, and as the evening approached, my mother prepared bowls filled with various foods. Each bowl had a lid with a hole cut in the center, and the challenge was for us kids to reach in, feel the food, and guess what it was without being able to see it. The foods included grapes in oil which felt like slimy eyeballs, a head of cauliflower covered on oil which felt like brains, links of sausage which felt like intestines. All my friends squealed in disgust and delight with each touch and there was a prize for each correct guess. The night was filled with pajamas, sleeping bags, scary movies, popcorn, and candy. Somehow, we managed to stay awake until sunrise every year and then slept the entire day away.

***

Brutus often suffered from a condition that I had little knowledge of - epilepsy. I would hear my mother scream, "Annie, its Brutus! I need your help!" I would come running to find Brutus laying on the floor convulsing. This was absolutely terrifying, and I knew it could lead to his death. I would kneel next to him and gently lay my upper body across him, as my mother instructed. It was in hopes of keeping him still enough to have my mother shove a pill down his throat. Once she got the pill down, she would get up and walk away. I was left lying across him, praying. Once his convulsions slowed down, I would lay behind him and slowly stroke his fur whispering that God was going to heal him and take away the seizures. The seizure would eventually cease, and Brutus was always left exhausted by the ordeal. Most nights my mother would keep him locked in the garage all night, despite my pleading her not too. I would never sleep well the nights of his seizures as I wondered if he was going to die alone in the darkness of the garage. I hated my mother for this, but if I tried to sneak him into the house, I feared she would get rid of him.

She often took joy in asking my friends when they came over to the house if they would like to take Brutus home with them. She stated, "Annie doesn't care about him, maybe you would. Annie is too stupid to care for a dog."

I begged her not to do this, but she was relentless. I could see my friend squirm in their seat and felt guilty they had to sit through this. My mother would state, "Let me just call your mom to ask if she will accept a dog into her home."

Usually, my friend would say, "I don't want a dog. I know my mom will say, ‘no’ anyways.”

My mother would pick up the phone and pretend she was talking to the parent on the other line. She would hang up and state, “Her mother will take him if you don’t follow through on your commitment to care of him.” It was a temporary relief to have that conversation end.

I was always in utter disbelief when she was in the middle of beating me, the phone would ring, and she would pause, and answer it with the sweetest voice, “Hello, can I help you?” It was incredibly confusing how her mood, affect and behavior would shift like a light switch. I would pray once she hung up, the pleasantries would continue. They never did.

“Now, where was I?” she would say as she saw me still bent over her bed with tear-stained cheeks. “Oh yes. Okay Annie let’s wrap this up.”

Sunday afternoons were filled with joy and happiness as that was the day I would go to my father’s house. He would pick me up after church and take me bowling or roller skating. Church was a very confusing experience for me as bible studies consisted of fear and threats. If you did anything to displease God, you were destined for Hell. I was taught that God was a vengeful God, waiting to pounce if you disobeyed any commandments or sinned against Him. In my heart, I did not believe this, and wanted to see Him as a loving and forgiving God. I had to believe this; I needed to believe this.

The pastor would come in and teach the last 10 minutes of Sunday School. I was always excited to share with him that I was going to my dad’s home after church. After months of sharing this excitement, the pastor took me by the shoulders, looked me in the eye, and stated, “I don’t care about you going to your dad’s home. I am sick and tired of you talking about your stupid father. If he really loved you, you would see him more than every Sunday.” I was devastated with tears welling up in my eyes, as I peered up at Paster Michael. He released my shoulders and started the bible lesson.

I told my father about this when he picked me up and we proceeded directly to the church instead of the bowling alley that day. He told me to wait in the car as I begged him not to go in. Ten minutes later he came out, got in the car, and said, “You ready to go bowling and have fun?”

I knew the pastor would share this with my mother, and I would be in big trouble. It was difficult to have fun that day as I could not stop worrying about Pastor Michael contacting my mother. My father sensed this fear and tried to soothe me.

I returned home that evening to find my mother sitting in the front hallway waiting for me. She happily informed me she received an interesting phone call from Pastor Michael this afternoon, and how my father threatened him.

Her joy left her face as she screamed, "How could you embarrass me in front of the church? How could you lie like that? Because of your actions, you will never see your father again!" She grabbed me by the arm, ushered me to the bathroom, and promptly shoved a bar of Ivory soap into my mouth. She screamed, "Bite down on it!" I bit down as she shoved it in and out of my mouth, making sure chunks of soap scrapped off onto my teeth.

She removed the bar and said, "Now chew the chunks and tell me you lied." I begged her to stop and that I was sorry. She continued, "Say you lied! Say you lied! You are such a liar, and liars go to Hell!"

I felt broken and finally muttered, "I lied, and I am so sorry."

She said, "I am calling a psychologist tomorrow and you are going to see him. You are a pathetic liar and I need to have you fixed before you go to Hell!" If it would make her feel better, I would happily see a psychologist. Maybe this doctor would actually help me and see I am not lying. Maybe he could make my mother understand.

The next week, I was ushered to a psychologist. He was very formal and somewhat intimidating. His breath smelled bad, and his office was musty. I found it exceedingly difficult to talk, but I eventually began to open up after he promised anything said to him would not be shared with my mother. I thought, if I did not tell him everything, he could not help me. And if he did not help me, I feared she would kill me someday. I told him everything, including the antique living room lamp I broke roughhousing with Brutus and clumsily glued back together. Towards the end of the session, he excused himself and stated he needed to speak with my mother in efforts to schedule another appointment. Ten minutes later, he came back in and stated I was free to go. I met my mother in the lobby, and she smiled and waved to the doctor as we left the office, while her grip around my forearm tightened.

We arrived home and I was punched so hard in the face that it knocked me off my feet. I laid on the floor looking up at my mother hovering over me. She was so angry that spit flew from her mouth as she yelled, "How could you? I spent $50 to have you fixed and all you did was lie to the doctor about me! How could you embarrass me like that?"

She bent down, grabbed a handful of hair, and jerked me up to my feet. "You finally admitted to breaking the lamp, but the rest are lies. You deserve everything you have coming to you. You are a stupid liar and God will punish you."

I was then ushered to the table and had a piece of paper and pencil thrust into my hand. She stated, "You will write an apology letter to the psychologist explaining that you lied, and you are sorry. After you are done with that, on a separate piece of paper you will write 'I am a pathetic liar and I will change for God's sake', one hundred times."

I trembled as I wrote the letter thinking to myself that writing this was a lie. I was telling the truth, and by stating I lied, was a lie. I was so confused and wondered why this was happening to me. 'Would God forgive me for lying, or was I truly headed to Hell?' Maybe I was already there. My mind wandered to hiking through the woods with Brutus and laying in the tree stand with Ralphie. I wanted to run, and as soon as I could, I would.

I finished the assignment and handed it to my mother. She yelled, "Not good enough!" I wrote the letter 'I' one hundred times down the paper, then 'am' one hundred times, and so on until the sentence was complete. I thought it was a clever way to complete the assignment without having to each sentence in full, one at a time. Somehow, she figured this out by the flow of my handwriting and stated, 'Now do it two hundred times the correct way. I do not care if it takes you all night, just get it done. You're such a liar, you can't even complete an assignment about lying without deception."

I wrote late into the night until I was finished. She seemed pleased with the end result, and I was then allowed to go to bed without dinner.

Click-click. Click-click. The summer train heading to a magical land; far, far away.

***

Jumping the creek, my little hand locked into my father's, was the highlight of my Sundays. After my father picked me up late Sunday mornings, we, without fail, stopped at Wood's Market & Gas. It was a small, wooden, red building with white awnings. The paint was peeling, which gave it an old Midwestern barn feel. The store had two gas pumps out front with a dilapidated sign reading, 'Get the best gas in town! Regular Unleaded .65$ and Super .71$'. Our mission was not to fill the car with gas but to fill a small paper bag with penny candy.

The candy bins started at the beginning of one aisle towards the front of the store and went all the way down at the back of the store. The overflowing bins rose from the floor to over my head. I could feel the saliva start to flow as I stood in the center of the aisle, eyes scanning the entire glorious display, mentally taking stock of how much candy I could cram to the very top of my paper bag. I always started at the candy buttons bin and placed two strips in my bag. Next was a Slo Poke, one Sugar Daddy Pop, five wax candies, two atomic fireballs, four Bit O Honey, one pack of Kings Candy Cigarettes, two Charms Lollipops, a box of Chiclets gum, and three Jaw Busters. The bag was now filled to the top, but I plopped down in the center of the aisle, crossed-legged, and rearranged the candy within the bag in hopes to make a little more room for a few Smarties. Nine times out of ten I was successful in my mission.

The next stop was Lake Park to walk along the creek, skip rocks downstream, and jump at its narrowest point. My heart boomed with anticipation with the mighty leap across the quickly flowing stream. To my 9-year-old eyes, the stream was a wild and raging river, spanning ten feet across and ten feet deep. It was filled with massive fishes, possibly sharks and man-eating barracudas. We would give ourselves a good twenty-foot running head start and sync our pace before leaping off the rocky edge. Just as I would feel my forward momentum lose stream half-way over the creek, my father's momentum would pick up the slack and carry us across to the other side. My hand would tighten its grip in his for the terror of being swallowed up by the depths of a sea was oh so real. I would giggle and breathe a sigh of relief when our feet found the solid ground, and immediately declared the need to do it again…and again.

For the most part, I enjoyed school. I was not in jeopardy of displeasing my mother, and I was able to converse with friends. My favorite part of the day was P.E. as I was extremely competitive. I was athletic, and it was my time to shine. I was always the first to reach the ceiling of the gym when climbing rope, even ahead of the boys. I completed the most sit-ups in one minute and I ran the quarter mile the fastest. Marie was a girly girl. She had long blonde hair and if she was not brushing it, she was twirling it between her fingers. She frequently wore pink lipstick and reapplied it throughout the day. She was tall and had long, slender legs. She was my main competitor in the long jump and the quarter mile, and she knew it. I thoroughly enjoyed beating Marie in most things daily. We never missed an opportunity to rub it in each other's faces when we won a race against each other. Our disgust for each other was mutual.

Marie was forced to sit next to me one day on the bus because it was the only seat open. She had just beaten me in the half-mile race that day and I was feeling especially irritated because of it. We sat turned as far away from each other as possible so that we were almost sitting back-to-back on the school bus seat. She had her cute little pink purse sitting between us, unzipped with all her stuff open for the world to see. I saw a wallet, her ugly pink lipstick, crumpled-up papers, and her hairbrush. My mind started working a mile a minute. I could steal something out of her purse as a punishment for beating me today, I thought. It would probably make her feel horrible to have something go missing, and I didn't care in the least. 'I'm going to take her wallet,' I thought, and I could burn it in the neighbor's trash pit this afternoon. My heart began to race at the thought of her catching me lifting her wallet out of her purse. She was getting off on the next bus stop, so I had to do it now. I held my breath and removed her wallet from her purse. I tucked it under my jacket as she prepared to exit the bus. My heartbeat pounded in my ears, and I wanted to throw up.

It was my turn to exit the bus, so I rushed inside my home and ran straight to my room. My mother was still at work, so no chance of her catching me with the wallet. I looked inside and saw a quarter, a picture of Marie in fifth grade, that's it. I left both items inside the wallet and headed outside and down the hill. Mr. Zasper was our next-door neighbor, and he had a large trash pit at the end of his property. He would burn his trash in that pit once a week, so if I threw the wallet in, it would get burned by week's end. But wait, what if someone found the wallet before he burned the trash? I would need to burn it in the pit today. But what if he saw the fire and came outside to investigate? What to do?

I decided to throw it in the pit, halfway covering it up with trash waiting to be burned. I thought that would be the best solution; I thought wrong. The days ticked by, and no fire yet. Maybe I should get it out and return it to Marie. Maybe I should just start the fire myself. What if he sees it? What if my mother sees it? The waiting was making me so anxious. Finally, the next day I saw the flames coming from Mr. Zasper's fire pit. I breathed a sigh of relief as I watched the flames dance through the pit.

The next day, Marie was still complaining about her missing wallet. I was torn between guilt and satisfaction. I came home that day from school to Mr. Zasper standing in my living room speaking with my mother. My mother asked me to step into the living room and join the conversation. My heart was officially lodged in my throat, and I felt like I was going to pass out.

My mother's arm lifted from her side, and in her hand was Marie's wallet. She and Mr. Zasper looked intently at me and asked if I knew whose wallet this was. I, without hesitation, stated, "No, I do not." Her smile left her face as Mr. Zasper uncomfortably shifted his weight.

"I am going to ask you again," she said, "and mind you, I already know the answer. Do you know whose wallet this is?"

My mind was at warp speed. Do I keep up the lie? Do I tell the truth? Which option will be less painful?

"Yes," I said. "It is Marie's wallet."

The silence hung in the room for what seemed like an eternity. Do I say more? Who is going to speak next? My mother told me to go to my room and she showed Mr. Zasper out the door. I waited and waited but she never came to my room. The anticipation was almost more than I could bare. I crawled into bed, pulled the covers up to my chin, clinched onto Ralphie under the covers, and prayed. My eyes grew heavy and before I knew it, it was morning. I got dressed for school and went downstairs.

My mother was making breakfast and smiled as she said, "Good morning."

I could not believe it. How did I not get punished for this?

Was it yet to come?

I finished breakfast and started to leave when she said, "I will pick you up from school today. When the bell rings, I will meet you out front." I thought that was strange but did not dare question it.

Right before lunchtime, Principal Mason instructed the schoolteachers to line the kids up outside, along the wall of the school. No one seemed to know why this was going on, but the students followed direction. We often did drills during school to prepare if a tornado were to hit. We lined up outside, along the wall, in the front of the school. I saw my mother's car parked in the parking lot facing the front of the school. I thought this was strange, as it was not the end of the day. She exited her car dressed in her police uniform, so I thought she was on her way to work. She motioned for me to come to the car. I followed her direction and starting walking towards the car. Once I reached her, she said to turn around and take a look at all the kids staring in our direction. The teachers seemed confused, but the principal told them to remain quiet. I stood there with my mother behind me, her hands on my shoulders and she whispered in my ear to remove my pants.

I turned my head to look up at her and she said again, "Remove your pants now."

I begged her not to do this, but she started unbuckling my jeans. She stated, "You embarrassed me in front of the psychologist and our neighbor, now it's your turn to be embarrassed."

She yanked my pants and underwear down, turned me around to face the hood of her car, and made me lay across the hood while she removed her police belt from her pants. Once removed, she began to beat me across my bare buttocks and thighs. I screamed for her to stop as Principal Mason ordered the kids back into the school.

The principal ran over and began yelling, "you told me this would be a police demonstration for the kids! What are you doing?"

My mother exclaimed, "This is a police demonstration of my daughter and her inability to tell the truth. Remember Principal Mason, the police are here to serve and protect you. It would be a shame if they didn't protect you anymore, wouldn't it?" The principal turned away and went back into the school.

The beating finally stopped as I tried to preserve any shred of dignity left while I pulled up my pants. I stumbled into the car and bent over trying not to vomit, praying not to vomit. My mother got into the car and said, "I hope this teaches you a lesson not to steal again." She began to rub my back and assure me everything would be okay. "I love you, Annie. I only do this because I love you".

With that, I opened the car door, hung out and vomited my lunch into the school parking lot.

***

On a Sunday in late summer, my father picked me up at his regular time and stated, "Annie, we are not going roller skating today, but we are going somewhere very special." I was instantly disappointed, as skating, with my father watching, was the highlight of my week.

"Dad, I don't want to go anywhere else."

He promised it would be great, and a day I would never forget. "We are going to a family reunion. It is my side of the family, and you will meet people who you have never met before."

Hmmm, my curiosity was peaked. "Okay, dad."

My father was married once before my mother and had two children, Kit and Ben. We often went to Kit's home on Sunday evenings for dinner which I enjoyed as she had three children, my niece and two nephews, who were close in age to me. Ben was married with two children; my other two nieces, and we sporadically went to their house for dinner as well. My father had two brothers, David, and Bill, and one sister, Ellen. Long before I was born, Uncle Bill died in World War II and received a Purple Heart for his service. His death wounded my father terribly. Aunt Ellen was wonderful, as she worked in Wood's Market & Gas as the cashier. We went to see her there every Sunday and she would always give me extra candy.

I only met my Uncle David once. I heard he won the Indiana lottery, and the family never heard from him again.

We arrived at the family reunion which was being held at Lake Park, and I did not see anyone I knew. I felt a little shy as people came up to my father and me, shaking hands and giving hugs. I saw a girl, wearing a pale blue dress, close to my age, but a few years older. She was playing alone, and I thought how nice it would be to play with her.

My father saw this little girl, and said, "Linda, come over here. I want you to meet someone."

Linda dropped the rocks she was playing with and met us by the large oak tree we were standing under. "Annie, this is Linda. She is your sister. Say 'hi' to her."

I looked up at my dad in utter confusion. This was not my sister. I had two sisters, and they were named Sandy and Louise.

"Annie, say hello to your sister!"

I looked at her long and hard; she had the same nose as my dad, the same stunning blue eyes. Why didn't I meet her before? Where does she live?

"Hello," I mumbled.

My father said, "Annie, is that the way to greet your sister?"

My brain was racing faster than I could keep up. I do not want another sister. I do not know her, and I do not want to know her, I screamed to myself. I turned and ran away. I wanted to run so far that my legs would have to fall off before I ever willfully stopped. I ended up on the outskirts of the park, sitting with my back against a weeping willow tree.

"He is my father. I won't share him with anyone else," I yelled at the tree. I stared at it half expecting it to speak back some words of wisdom, but they never came.

My father eventually found me, took my hand, and pulled me to my feet. "You will go and say you are sorry, and then I am taking you home," he announced.

I reluctantly followed suit, as he ushered me along with a tight grip on my hand back to the party. "I'm sorry," I said in the most defiant way I could muster up, without any eye contact.

And with that, it would be years before I saw my sister Linda again.

Chapter Four

"The hard days are what make you stronger."

~ ***Aly Raisman***

The next few months before winter was long and depressing. I was still reeling from the embarrassment at school. I lost many friends as they did not know how to deal with what they witnessed. The teachers did not speak to me much, as I think they feared any misconstrued comments would set off my mother. Her dirty cop boyfriends would continue to come in and out of the house. They did not bother me much, and I liked their presence as it seemed to put my mother in a good mood. Any attention off me was good attention.

My mother worked nights at Lakeside Steel as a police officer after she lost her job with the Chester police department. She would leave soon after dinner and Louise was left in charge of me. Louise had no desire to be responsible for her younger sister, and she made that abundantly clear at every opportunity. I would leave notes for my mother before I went to bed asking if I could wear pants or a skirt to school the next morning, since she would be asleep. I got myself off to school in the morning and did so as quietly as possible to not wake her. She would drink herself into oblivion after work because I would find the empty bottles in the morning.

I'm not sure if it was the influence of alcohol, her untreated bipolar disorder, or her traumatic childhood that caused her to spiral into fits of anger followed by bouts of depression. She was found one afternoon sitting in the corner of her bedroom with her work-issued rifle loaded and the barrel in her mouth. From that day forward, she often told me she did not pull the trigger because she had children to raise, and how grateful we should all be that she did not kill herself. The guilt bestowed upon me at every turn was like the barrel of a shotgun in my mouth. There were days I wished she had pulled the trigger.

Winter was now in full swing and for Christmas, I received new snow skis. Every winter I would inevitably break a ski and every Christmas I was gifted a new pair. Once we had our first big snowfall, I was out at the bottom of the hill building a huge ramp out of snow. Once the ramp was as tall as I could build it, I went into the house and got a large bucket of chilly water. I placed the heavy bucket on the toboggan and slowly lowered it to the ramp since it was too heavy to carry through the snow.

I poured the water all over the snow ramp which compacted the snow. I then put another layer of snow on top. I repeated this process until the ramp was compacted and frozen. I could not wait until school the next day to tell my friends that the ramp was ready. The following Saturday, it seemed like the whole neighborhood was gathering in my driveway to take their turn skiing down our hill and off the strategically placed ramp. We spent hours outside sledding and skiing until it was dark, and the streetlights came on; the universal sign for all kids to get home immediately.

The next few weekends were filled with skiing, sledding, ice skating, building snow tunnels and igloos. Brutus and I would make snow angels and catch snowflakes on our tongues. Brutus would patiently wait for the family of white-tailed deer to come out and feast on the salt licks at the end of the property. After a few attempts of trying to catch them at the beginning of the winter, he gave up and reluctantly sat to watch them.

I loved spending time in the winter at my best friend Trish's home, as there was a long winding stream that ran two acres behind her house. We would start mid-morning, headed from her home to the frozen wonderment of that stream. We placed our ice skates on the bright red sled she had and pulled them behind us on our way to skate. Once we reached the ice, we transferred into our skates and became professional ice skaters.

We dreamed we were Dorothy Hamill and Peggy Fleming doing toe loops, double axels, and death spirals. We glided across the ice as the wind rushed past our frozen ears. We moved with such grace, such ease until we did not. Our outings were filled with more horizontal time on the ice than vertical. We giggled with each fall and helped each other back to our feet. I would trip over the occasional frog frozen half under the ice, and half above it. We would lay on our bellies, staring quizzically at the top half of the unfortunate frog; its eyes glazed over with ice. "I wonder if he is alive," Trisha asked. "Maybe," I said. "If so, I wonder what he's thinking." With that, we were back on our feet and back to our Olympic competition.

We spent hours on that wide stream, dreaming, exploring, and being free. Free from worry, free from expectations, just free. The light was growing dim, so it was time to head back to Trisha's house. We must have seen it at the same time, as we both stopped dead in our tracks and grabbed each other's hand.

"Don't move," I said. "If we run, it will attack us." I had a tough time hearing the words leave my mouth as my heart was pounding like a drum. The creature had locked eyes with us, its ears alert and poised to take off at any sudden movement. The seconds stretched on as we stood frozen in its gaze, but in reality, it was only a matter of minutes.

"Okay, let's stay together and start walking very slowly," I whispered. Our bodies, stuck together like glue, slowly made our way to the frozen ground.

"Wait," I said, "he is no longer looking at us." In fact, he had not moved a muscle. His gaze was still fixated on the spot we originally saw him. "I think he is frozen Trish." We walked a little further, still no movement.

We gained the courage to approach the wild dog. As we circled behind him, still, no movement. We were now standing face-to-face with the incredibly tall animal. His ear tips met the base of our chin, and his fur was matted down, frozen with ice crystals on the tip of his nose. "How can a dog just freeze to death like that?" We had never seen anything like it. The fear was soon replaced with sorrow.

"What if he was someone's pet?" I asked Trisha.

She responded, "There are many wild dogs around here. I'm sure it was no one's pet. My dad says they are mean and aggressive and would not hesitate to rip your throat out if they wanted to."

With that, I shuttered and ushered her away from the spot, so we could head home.

I was woken from a deep slumber by being yanked out of bed and dragged to the floor. My mother hovered over me and screamed, "You didn't flush the toilet again! I am done!" There was a small bathroom across the hallway from my bedroom. If I got up in the middle of the night and had to relieve myself, I did but never flushed at night. One night I flushed the toilet which happened to be above my mother's bedroom. This woke her up and she beat me in her drunken stupor. She had not remembered this and told me to flush the toilet from now on. Every night, I stood in front of the toilet debating whether I should flush, or not flush. I knew she told me to, but she beat me last time I did, so every night, I decided it was best not to flush.

The next morning was the straw that broke the camel's back. She hovered over me demanding I remove my nightgown. I, true to form, begged her not to beat me.

"You are so pathetic. Pathetic little Annie, begging for mercy. If you just had flushed the toilet, you would not be in trouble." she said and grabbed me by the hair and dragged me over to the toilet. She held my head over the toilet and told me to drink the water. I refused, and at that point did not care if she beat me. I would not drink that water; she would have to kill me first. Out of her frustration, she dragged me down the stairs by my hair and opened the front door. She placed her hand on my back and shoved me out the front door, naked, into the large snow drift. She closed the door, and I heard it lock behind her. I then saw the front drapes be pulled closed.

Do I leave the snow drift to pound on the door and risk someone seeing me naked, or do I stay in the protection of the drift? My fingers and toes became so cold I could no longer feel them. I decided to risk being seen and started pounding on the front door. It was hard making a fist as I could not feel my fingers. I pounded and with each strike on the door, it felt like electricity pulsed through my fingers. Finally, the door opened, and I was allowed inside.

"Get dressed. You are so pathetic." I scrambled upstairs and put on as many clothes as I could find. I crawled into my closet, shut the door, and hid. I sat in the dark and prayed I would be magically transported to another family. But only if I could take Brutus and Ralphie.

***

The day came that I found myself in an orthodontist's chair staring at metal bands and wires about to be inserted into my reluctant mouth. The orthodontist had the personality of a wet carpet. His monotone voice, with a cigarette-smelling breath was enough to increase my anxiety a few ticks. He placed the first metal band on top of my bottom front tooth. He then picked up what looked like a rubber mallet and placed it on top of the hovering metal band. I thought to myself, *This cannot be good.*

The last step was the tool that looked like a hammer. *Okay, this was getting worse by the second.* He raised the hammer instrument and struck the rubber mallet-looking instrument, which drove the metal ring down my tooth and into the gum. The first strike did not quite sink the metal ring deep enough under my gums, so another smack was in order. The tears began to flow down my cheeks, and I looked at him with pleading eyes.

He stated, "Great. Twenty-three more to go."

I thought to myself, '*this cannot be the real way braces happen. He must be doing this wrong. Is he a real orthodontist? Why do people volunteer to do this?*'

All questions I could not verbalize as there were mallets, hammers, and metal in my mouth. Not to mention, questioning an adult leads to a guaranteed punishment. I wiggled in that seat as if I had fire ants in my pants.

I could tell his patience was wearing thin, and he sternly barked, "Stop it! It does not hurt that bad! You are over-exaggerating! Keep it up and I will tell your mother not to bring you back here."

Once the torture was over, I leaped up from the chair and almost passed out from the pain and sudden rush of blood from my head. I looked back at the dental tool tray, and it looked like an animal sacrifice had taken place. My heartbeat was felt in every tooth in my mouth and my gums felt like raw hamburger meat.

My mother showed compassion by stopping at Dairy Queen on the way home and getting me a strawberry milkshake. The cold on my gums provided merciful, temporary relief. I laid my head against the seat rest and focused on the warm sunshine spilling in through the car window.

"You know Annie," she said, "those braces are awfully expensive. I asked your father to help pay for them, but he refused."

My head knew where this was going, but my heart refused the believe. "If he loved you, he would help pay for these braces. He obviously does not love you, so I have to pay the full amount." She continued, "If you do not want to see him this Sunday, I will be happy to call him and tell him you do not feel well."

Could he really have refused to pay because he did not love me? I thought he loved me, but now I was not so sure. Why would my mother lie to me? It must be true if she said it. "Sure mom. You can call him and tell him." With that, she patted my knee with her hand and said, "I will take care of you. When no one else loves you, I do."

After three Sundays passed with my refusal to see my father, the following Sunday he showed up at the front door. My mother saw it was him and refused to open it. She yelled, "Annie, your loser father is at the front door. If you do not want to talk with him, I will tell him to go away."

I ran down and opened the door. I did not care if he did not love me, I loved him and I wanted to be with him today. I got in the car, and we drove off down the road.

"Dad," I asked, "why didn't you love me enough to help pay for my braces"?

He pulled the car over, turned off the ignition, and shifted his body to face me. "Annie, I paid the orthodontist in full for your braces. Your mother did not pay a penny towards your braces. I love you more than my own life and will always be there for you and your needs."

The hot tears came flowing from my eyes as I threw my arms around his neck. "Oh daddy, I love you too. I am so sorry I did not see you for three weeks. I thought you didn't love me anymore."

I have never seen my father have tears in his eyes before, but today I did.

Chapter Five

"Out of suffering have emerged the strongest souls; the mostmassive characters are seared with scars."

~ ***Khalil Gibran***

I entered middle school that next Fall and started to dislike it. I struggled to keep up my grades and every report card sent home had the same remarks written by the teachers; 'Annie is a daydreamer. She stares at the clock all day and has difficulty focusing. She is a social butterfly and disrupts class often due to talking.'

I thought the more I talked, the more people would like me. I needed people to like me, as I did not like myself. I did not care about classwork or grades; I needed to be needed. I needed to belong. I needed to be loved.

I skated by the first year of middle school and was barely promoted to the next year. My mother came home one day and told me she lost her job, and we would be moving to Florida. Florida?

After all the time and effort I put into having people like me here in Indiana? No, no way. What about my father? Is he coming? She made a noble attempt at trying to get me comfortable with this decision. She promised we would have Dairy Queen every day and we would swim in the Gulf of Mexico every weekend. I found myself growing fond of the idea and eventually became excited about the upcoming move.

She said, "Oh yeah, we need to give away Brutus before the move, which will be in two weeks."

What? Give away Brutus? No, no way. I protested with every ounce of my being. She stated, "It's not fair taking an Alaskan Malamute to a hot climate. We must give him away." I told her no one would want him being 9 years old and needing medication daily for epilepsy. I pulled out all the stops. I pleaded, begged, cried, offered to work, and offered anything I could think of to make her change her mind.

She stated, "It's final. He is going as soon as I find someone to take him. This is for the best."

The best? Whose best? Not mine.

***

The next two weeks were the longest of my life. I hated her. I hated my life. I especially hated Florida and I was not even there yet. I spent every free minute with Brutus, loving him, petting him, talking to him, and especially apologizing to him. I promised him I would think of him every day until we were back together. I promised him as soon as I was old enough to get a car, I would drive back to Indiana, find him and we would find our own home, together. He knew, as he always knew what I was saying to him. He gently licked the tears from my cheeks and placed his paw on my shoulder.

The day eventually came when it was time to go. The movers would arrive later in the day to pack our things and drive our belongings to Florida. Brutus was still at home with us; I dare not ask, but I guess he would be coming in the car and driving to Florida with us. I anxiously anticipated all of us getting into the car. If I had him, all would be okay. I was told to get into the car which was parked in the garage, and I did. Brutus was still tied up on his leash in the garage. I smiled at him knowing he would come with us. He had to be coming with us. My mother patted him on the head as she made her way into the car. She got in and turned the ignition.

I finally asked, “Why isn’t Brutus in the car? What is going on?”

She responded, “The movers will take him home with them, no worries.” I could not speak; it was as if my voice box were removed. We pulled out of the driveway, I screamed, “Stop! I need to say goodbye.”

She said, “There is no time. We must go.”

“Please! Please! Stop for one minute!” I pressed my face against the glass window as tears rolled down my eyes. Brutus was dancing in circles, still tied to his leash anchored to the garage wall. We slowly pulled down the drive and that was the last time I ever saw my best friend.

The pain was almost unbearable. My heart was shattered into a million pieces. The grief was beyond comprehension. How could this happen? What would happen to him? How would I ever find him again? I promised him I would be with him again, but how could I if I did not know who took him? So many questions, no answers.

The 1,300-mile trip, riding in the back of a 1980 Firebird Formula with a broken heart was the longest two days of my life. Ralphie was my only faithful companion now. I stroked his clumped fur as if it were Brutus and whispered words of love into his ear. Laying in the backseat, I watched the tops of trees zoom by as we barreled down I65. The puffy clouds hung high in the crystal blue sky. It took me back to Brutus and I lying in the soft, green grass watching the clouds float by as they morphed into tigers, mountains, lizards, and ice cream cones. Sometimes, a plane so high in the sky looked like the head of a pin would disappear into our magical clouds and emerge out the other end.

I was jolted out of my daydream with my mother screaming, “Annie, look at the Smoky Mountains!”

It was as if the road was carved out right through the center of the mountains. The rock walls on either side of the road were rugged and climbed higher than my eyes could view out the tiny car window. The layers of sandstone, slate, granite, and limestone rock alternated in colors from deep brown, light brown, charcoal grey, and shimmering brick red. If straining my neck, I could faintly see yellow birch and basswood trees standing tall like soldiers at the top of the rock wall. The winding, mountainous road was breathtaking and awe-inspiring. It was as if I was in a different world, a new dimension filled with grace and beauty. Maybe this would be a new beginning. A beginning of joy, peace, and forgiveness for a mother filled with rage and pain, and a daughter mortally wounded, but hopeful.

We finally reached our destination in South Florida. The June heat was suffocating and the sun on my skin felt like standing too close to a space heater. My eldest sister, Sandy ran out her front door and happily greeted me and my mother, "Welcome to sunny Florida!" We stayed with Sandy for a couple of days until the movers delivered our belongings from Indiana. We then moved into the other side of Sandy's duplex. Sandy and her husband owned a beautiful duplex situated on a road called Sunshine Way.

We settled in and tried to acclimate to the heat, little lizards, and flying cockroaches. There were small lizards by the hundreds, geckos, red-sided Curly tail lizards, Large-headed Anole, Six-lined Racerunners, and Skinks. It was like entering a world of miniature dinosaurs. I spent endless hours chasing these fast-moving, elusive lizards. If I got close enough to grab one, my fear made me hesitate right before I made contact. I finally obtained the courage one sultry day to reach out and grab one. I felt it wiggle furiously in my hand as I held it loosely, trying not to crush it. Once it finally settled down and I only felt a small wiggle, I slowly opened my hand and looked eye-to-eye with the brown-stripped lizard. He was not moving, but his tail was moving. His tail was no longer attached to its body! It looked like a tiny snake slithering but staying in place at the same time. I dropped the lizard and its tail then screamed in panic and guilt. Sandy ran outside and asked what was wrong.

I told her I broke the lizard's tail because it fell off. Tears flowed down my face, "I didn't mean to hurt it! Is it going to die?" I asked.

Sandy took me in her arms and said, "Annie, it won't die. When those lizards get scared, they detach their tails, so predators attack the tail and not them."

"Really?" I said. Sandy said the tails grow back and will have a full-grown tail within the next couple of months. I breathed a sigh of relief knowing I did not kill the lizard, and realized I was on a big learning curve in this unfamiliar territory.

We had our first encounter with a flying cockroach the third night in our new home. Our home only had one bedroom, so my mother and I had to share. She slept on her bed, while I slept on a small futon that we kept in the basement in Indiana. The bedroom was pitch black at night and I could not even see my hand held in front of my face. I woke at 3am to the sound of something moving around. It sounded like something with wings flying around the bedroom. As the noise grew louder, I knew whatever was in the room was close to me and as the sound lessened, it was further away from me. I pulled the covers over my head and prayed whatever was trapped in our bedroom was friendly and did not bite.

I whispered, "Mom, wake up. Something is in our bedroom." Silence.

"Mom! Wake up." My voice grew louder and louder, and I imagined this flying object was getting more agitated with each increased octave of my voice.

"What!" my mother yelled. She finally became aware of the flying object in our room.

She flipped the light on, and with blurry eyes, we saw what looked like the size of a small bat flying around the room. Flying cockroaches only fly for short distances, and then must land for a period before they take flight again. We both let out a blood curdling scream loud enough to wake Sandy on the other side of the duplex. As the tail-end of the scream left our mouths, the cockroach then landed on my foot that barely exposed outside of my covers. I felt the tiny legs wiggle on the top of my foot which sent chills from my toes up to my scalp. I flailed my foot so hard it sent the cockroach flying across the room and land on my mother's bed up by her head.

I jumped, more like flung myself from my bed, across the room so hard I slammed into the door. I threw the door open and ran out into the living room screaming then rubbing my foot as if to get poison off my skin. Sandy pounded on the front door yelling to open the door and let her in. We opened the door and could not get the words out fast enough.

"The bedroom! The flying thing! My foot! Landed!" my mother and I uttered.

Sandy, lover of all creatures large and small, found the cockroach, scooped it into a Tupperware container and released it outside. I stood there with my mouth hanging open. Sandy, my brave, big sister just caught a flying menace to society and released it outside, to see another day.

"What if it comes back? I want to go back to Indiana NOW!" I exclaimed.

That summer was full of adventures, but also full of loneliness. I missed my friends, I missed my father, and I mostly missed my beloved Brutus. I thought of him every day and wondered what he was doing. If he was cared for. If he hated me for leaving him. In the location we lived, no other children seemed to be playing outside that summer, so I needed to entertain myself. My mother bought me a bike which gave me freedom to explore the small town. I frequently found myself at the community park next door to the middle school in hopes to meet another kid and make a friend. I was the only one there most days, in the sweltering heat of the summer. I sat on the swing, the only sound was the wind gently flowing across the playground towards the school parking lot.

The air smelled of rotten eggs from the city water and the only sound I could hear was the wind blowing the snap hook on the school flagpole against the metal pole. The flag was safely stored away in the summertime while school was out. I was so lonely, felt so isolated and could not wait for the school year to begin. The storm clouds would roll in from the east at 2pm everyday like clockwork. The sky would look ominous as the large, black clouds moved across the sky. In the distance, the water poured out of the clouds like grey curtains onto the earth. Meanwhile, I sat in the sunshine watching the storm roll in. I became proficient in knowing when I needed to head for home before the rain would reach my house.

The afternoon storms only lasted about 45 minutes, and after they passed, the steam rising off the hot pavement would fill the city streets. It looked like the streets were on fire, but without the red flames. Post storm, the sun would shine, and the air was humid and heavy. The air felt thick and wet as it entered the lungs. I would run outside after the storm and search for the rainbow. There would always be a rainbow, sometimes a double rainbow. I would look in awe and wondered where the rainbow ended. Was there really a pot of gold at the end, or was that just made up? Did double rainbows mean two pots of gold? Someday I would find the end and determine for myself.

Little did I know that our current residence was a temporary one. My mother found a condo across town situated in a golf course community. She wanted us to move before the school year started so I would be enrolled in the school located close to our community. The condo had four units and she choose the upper, east-side unit. It was a beautiful community, filled with tall palm trees, lakes, an 18-hole golf course and swimming pools behind each condo. I was excited to move into the condo as I would finally have my own bedroom, and I could swim in a crystal blue swimming pool whenever I wanted.

There were at least ten small lakes throughout the community, and on the edge of the lake, numerous signs were posted reading, 'Do not swim. Alligators may be in water.' I thought I would be the judge of that. Alligators are slow-moving animals that are afraid of humans...or so I thought. In the summer, there were no golfers out on the course. I walked the course daily, right down the middle of the fairways, through sand traps, making pit stops at the small restroom facilities that were located all over the course for water and bathroom breaks. I took immense joy in walking barefoot through the lush, soft green grass and sugar sand in the traps.

Once season was in full swing, around December, I swam in the pool daily to collect golf balls that were resting at the bottom of the pool. It was wise to always be on guard while at the pool, as novice golfers hit misguided golf balls into buildings, pools, and lakes. Every weekend, I pool hopped all over the community to collect as many balls as I could find. This was tricky, since each pool had a gate around it and a lock only immediate residents had a key to. This meant I had to jump the fence without being caught. Once I gathered as many golf balls as I could find, I took them to the pro-shop. I carried them in a large bucket, struggling under the weight while still dripping wet in my bathing suit.

The nice man behind the counter would pay me five cents per ball, and always say, "how about you dry off before entering the pro-shop?" Every time I promised I would next time I came in, but I always forgot with the excitement of being paid for my arduous work. The payment was totally worth the risk of being busted in a pool I was not allowed to use.

***

School started at the end of August which seemed so early compared to the North. The first day of school was filled with excitement and anxiety as I was the new kid on the block. It was a culture shock for me, since I was from a small town in the Midwest and was now a minority in a predominantly Hispanic school. Many kids spoke Spanish in the hallways between classes, so I never quite understood what they were saying. I thought to myself that it was going to be difficult making friends if I did not know how to converse with them. I suppose I looked lonely, when a girl walked up to me at lunch and asked to sit with me. She was new to the school as well and was looking for a friend. I eagerly slid over in my seat, so she could sit down.

"Hi. My name is Tammy," she said.

I told her my name, and within 5 minutes, we were best friends. Her parents had a huge RV that they took to Lake Placid in the summertime. I became a frequent companion of Tammy during their trips where we swam, waterskied, and giggled at the good-looking boys. If I was not at her house on the weekends, she was at mine. Tammy was unlike any friend I ever had. She was my best friend, but she frequently ended our relationship for no apparent reason. I lived in a constant state of anxiety that I would do or say something wrong that would make her upset and end our friendship. These were the days that my people-pleasing skills were in high gear.

The older I became, the more my mother became verbally abusive. She would still punch me, slap me, and push me into walls, then rip out clumps of hair, but that seemed to wane as my stature met hers. She quickly met a man after moving to our new condo named Tony. Tony had two children, one boy and one girl. I tried to like Tony, but there was something creepy about him and the way he looked at me. He smoked cigars on our porch daily which would fill the condo with disgusting smoke. I would lock myself in my room to avoid the smell, but my mother saw this as a direct defiance to being nice and social.

One day, when she reached the end of her short fuse, she kicked the door in to my bedroom. She snatched me off my bed, slammed me against the wall and hissed, "You are not going to ruin this for me! I love Tony, we will marry one day if you don't screw it up for me." Spit sprayed onto my face as she held my shirt collar clenched in her fists. "You are a nasty, stupid, little bitch that is destined to bring me down. I will not let you! Do you hear me?"

I nodded and was told to get out in the living room now and talk to Tony. I walked out into the living room, wiping the spit off my face with the collar of my stretched-out shirt.

My mother said, "Oh Annie, there you are! Join us sweetheart and tell Tony about your day."

I felt like vomiting all over them both. My mother's ability to turn from sadistic to sappily sweet in a moment's notice was nauseating. I sat down, tried to paste a smile on my face, as Tony salivated while looking me up and down, his eyes feasting on my body. *Couldn't my mother see this? Did she care?*

I was a scrawny thirteen-year-old with glasses and braces. I was totally flat-chested and took very little time or interest in my appearance. I climbed trees, caught lizards, and played baseball. It made it more confusing to have a forty-five-year-old man looking at me the way he did. I just wanted to avoid him, and his two creepy children that visited on weekends.

Soon, she joyfully announced that she and Tony would be tying the knot in just a few weeks.

"Isn't that great sweetheart? You know, it is important to me that you like who I marry. Are you okay with this?" she asked.

I quickly weighed the consequences of telling the truth. Do I lie and condone this marriage made in hell, or do I tell the truth? She fooled me by genuinely seeming interested in my feelings. I rolled the dice and told her the truth.

"I don't like him. I do not want you to marry him. The way he looks at me makes me uncomfortable."

With that, my face met the floor. She hit me so hard I felt my teeth rattle in my head.

"You are hateful and just want me to be miserable like you" she seethed. "What do you expect when you parade around in your bathing suit all day? Of course, he is going to look at you!" She finished with, "We will marry whether you like it or not, and you will be at the wedding."

I looked at her with such hatred and contempt. I wanted to claw her eyes out and make her hurt as much as she hurt me. I was not strong enough yet, but one day I would be.

She and Tony were both dressed in grey on their wedding day. I found it quite fitting as it was a depressing day for me. They were so happy and so in love. It was them against the world, and no one would stand in the way of their happiness. I successfully avoided them and his children for most of the day and found a quiet spot in the dancehall to celebrate my solitude. A limo whisked them away at the end of the day to their honeymoon. Five days without them was my reward for this disgusting and dysfunctional union.

The end of the hurricane season brought my first experience with a tropical storm. The news stated it was going to be a rain maker with minimal wind damage. We decided to stay in our condo and weather out the storm. It was met with excitement and anticipation as it meant no school for a day or two. The storm hit late afternoon, and it rained just as promised by the weathercaster. It rained and rained and did not seem to let up for hours. We decided to go to bed and try to get some sleep. I woke up to my mother bursting into me bedroom yelling, "Look outside!" I got to my feet, opened the bedroom blinds, and could not believe my eyes.

People were canoeing and kayaking down our street, our street! The cars in the parking lot had water up to the hoods and grass was not visible as far as the eye could see. It was just water, and more water. We ran outside and down the front stairs but stopped two steps shy of the ground as the water was overtaking the stairs. The downstairs neighbors were yelling and frantic that water had breached into their condos and was ruining their carpets and furniture. We offered for them to come up to our condo, but they wanted to stay put and try to save their belongings.

We went back upstairs, sat on my bedroom floor, and gazed out the full-length window in total disbelief. We saw our first alligator and it was swimming down the street as people in canoes kept their distance. I couldn't believe what I was seeing, so I had to rub my eyes and take another look outside to confirm that it was real. I could never, even in my wildest dreams, think I would ever see an alligator swimming down a main thoroughfare. But there it was, slowly making its way from one end of the street to the other.

It took a few days for the water to fully recede and for the schools to reopen. The streets were filled with palm fronds, mulch, and dirt. Businesses were closed trying to recover from water damage. Gas stations and grocery stores were quick to reopen and service customers. We drove around town to see the damage that the storm inflicted. On our drive, I saw a 'Now Hiring' sign in the window of a fast-food restaurant. I thought to myself that I wanted a car in three years when I turned 16 years old, and I knew I would need to buy one myself.

Two days later, I hopped on my bike and went to the restaurant and asked for an application. I was handed one and sat in a booth to complete. I was shaking as I trying to answer questions, I was not sure the answers too. *What was my social security number? What was a W-2?*

As I was writing, the manager came out and slid into the booth facing me. He asked what hours and what days I could work. I told him that any day after school and weekends, and with that, he held out his hand to shake mine, and said, "You're hired."

I could not believe my ears. He said, "Come in tomorrow at 3pm and I will give you a uniform".

I walked out and felt like I was walking on air. A job! My first real job! Sure, I babysat often for two years, but I was going to make big money at this job, \$3.35 per hour! My first day on the job was the longest 5 hours of my life. I worked hard mopping floors, frying French fries and hush puppies, and mixing large vats of coleslaw with plastic gloves that reached up to my arm pits. I walked out at the end of my shift and sat on the stoop on the side of the building where my bike was chained up.

I stank like fish, frying oil, and dirty mop water. I had tiny burns up both arms from standing in front of the large fryer as food was cooking in boiling oil. I sat for a while before I could get up the energy to make the seven-mile bike ride home.

I made it home and carried my bike upstairs as I always did and placed it outside our front door against a metal railing. My mother frequently told me I needed to lock my bike to the railing, or it may be stolen. I got into the shower and washed the gross stink of the day off me. It took two rounds of shampoo to get the smell of oil out. I got dressed and my mother called me to come outside. I met her on the front porch, and she angrily asked why I had not locked my bike to the railing.

I knew there would not be a correct answer, so I stated, "I forgot."

"Well," she said, "hopefully, this will make you remember."

With that, she picked up my ten-speed, held it over her head and threw it off the second-floor balcony. The bike smashed onto the ground, bent the front rim, and busted off the seat.

"If you want the responsibility of a bike, earn it."

Mr. Calven, our downstairs neighbor came running out to see what the commotion was. My mother said, "Good afternoon, Mr. Calven! Annie needs to be more careful with her property. Sorry if she disturbed you."

I ran down the steps and examined my bike as Mr. Calven's eyes boar a hole through the back of my head.

"Annie, that could have killed me if I was outside!"

I apologized to Mr. Calven and told him I would be more careful next time. I looked up at my mother looking over the railing as the smile grew across her face.

"That's right Annie," she said, "you will be more careful next time."

It took what felt like 5,000 shifts at the restaurant to earn enough money to buy another bike. During this period, I had to walk to work which took much longer than riding a bike. I went down to the local K-Mart and bought myself a new ten-speed bike and still had a little money left over. I proudly rode it home and ran upstairs to show my mother. She came out to look at it, and said, "nice."

Then she turned around and went back inside. No 'good job,' 'nice work,' proud of you,' nothing. The disappointment hung around my neck like a noose. The eternal hope to please my mother and made her proud of me was like trying to nail Jell-O to a wall; impossible.

Chapter Six

"Life is never fair, and perhaps it is a good thing for most of us that it is not."
~ ***Oscar Wilde***

The last two years of middle school were boring and filled with drama. My first entire year of middle school was a repeat of my last year of school up north. It was tedious, and I found a tough time paying attention. Due to this, I frequently got in trouble that year with numerous notes from teachers coming home to my mother. 'Annie is not paying attention, talks constantly to others and is not easily redirected.' My mother did not seem to care too much, as she was more focused on her year-long marriage to Tony falling apart. It ended one night in an explosive fight between Tony and my mother, with Tony grabbing his belongings and walking out the door.

Seeing that, I felt absolute joy that loser was no longer going to be in my home, and absolute fear that all her anger and attention would now be laser-focused back to me. A few days later, all four of my mother's car tires were flat after 'someone' stuck a knife into them. I stood in my bedroom window, looking down on her in the parking lot, screaming at her car as if it was the car's fault. It was with great joy I saw my mother hurt by someone else's actions.

She screamed into the air, "I will get you Tony, if it's the last thing I do!"

The next boyfriend came soon after Tony left, which was a relief to me. This one seemed to leave me alone, made my mother happy, and diverted her attention from me; win-win. My first boyfriend came about the same time. His name was Pablo, and he was in most of my classes in school. He lived a few miles from me and introduced me to his Hispanic culture; the foods, the music and his tight-knit family. I was so smitten with Pablo and his kind, gentle nature. He would wait for me outside of the restaurant to finish my shift, so I would not have to ride my bike home alone. Weekends were full of swimming, tennis, movies and sneaking kisses. He was my first real kiss and my first real crush. We dated throughout seventh grade until he broke my heart by going out on a date with Jessica Messcot. She was tall, thin, with long brown hair, and at the top of our class. I knew I could not compete with her, so I resigned myself to a broken heart.

My eight-grade year was a year of increased confidence and exploration. I finally got my braces off, started using contacts instead of glasses, and my skin cleared up. I started working at a different fast-food restaurant and with that, earned .30 cents more an hour. My new best friend, Jenny taught me how to smoke cigarettes. We often snuck out of her house at night when I slept over and walked the streets smoking cigarettes we stole from her dad. I hated the taste, and it made me cough with every inhale, but it made me feel cool and older than my age.

Tammy and I stayed close throughout middle school and even into our first year of high school, but our bond gradually weakened as I found other friends who allowed me to be my true self. It came to a screeching halt when we planned on going to Freshman Homecoming together, but when I was offered something better, I cancelled on her. I fell into a group of friends that loved to drink alcohol, smoke cigarettes and skip school.

The week before my freshman year of high school began, my friend, Tanya and I joined the Marching Band. The first practice was held in the high school parking lot, and we were both more nervous than a long-tailed cat in a room full of rocking chairs. The incoming freshmen huddled together, and the upper-class students were like bloodhounds sniffing out the weakest link. Practice was every evening, and three mornings a week before class. We needed to be in our seats at 7:05am, so practice started at 5:30am SHARP. The band teacher was an ex-military marine core drill Sergeant. He was a tall, muscular man with dark skin and intense eyes that seemed to bore right through you. Standing at attention for minutes on end in the parking lot two hours before the sun came up was torture. Mosquitoes swarmed around our heads and buzzed in our ears. They bit our legs, our arms, our faces, through our clothes, up our noses, and if they could, they would bite our eyeballs. Mr. Maywell stood on a 20-foot podium that faced us while at attention.

He barked, "Welcome to the feast. These mosquitoes are my friends and under my control. If I ever see one of you attempt to swat, maim, injure, or kill one of my friends, I will see you, and come for you."

We believed him. We all believed him.

Two weeks into practice, I kept my eyes focused on Mr. Maywell's darting eyes. He was just waiting for one of us to flinch while at attention. The mosquitoes were particularly relentless this morning and one landed on the cease of my inner elbow. The burning and discomfort as he seemed to suck all the blood from my upper body became more than I could bare. I waited for his eyes to pass me by as he was scanning, and I turned my arm slowly inward to rub it against the side of my waist. And just like that, Mr. Maywell jumped off the podium and began running through the sea of students frozen in attention.

No, I thought. There is no way he could have seen me. He must have seen someone else. He made his way closer and closer to me, weaving his way like a linebacker with a ball navigating the defensive line. My heart began to pound faster and faster.

Before I knew it, he was one inch from my face. Nose to nose as he crouched down to my level. "So. Ms. Williams, you decided to try your luck and attack my friend", he snarled. His breath was hot on my face and the smell of sweat was pungent. "What do you have to say for yourself?"

My brain was frozen in fear, and my mouth felt welded shut. "I..I..I.. don't know", I mustered.

"Well, I don't know is not an answer, so as your punishment you will run laps around my parking lot until I tell you to stop."

I was thrilled. I would have a greater chance keeping mosquitoes off me while running than just standing still at attention. I was able to reserve my excited expression and took off running laps.

"Now is there anyone else that would like to join Ms. Williams on her morning run?"

It did not surprise me that no one spoke up.

I grew to have such respect and admiration for Mr. Maywell. He demanded respect, and every student in that band gave it to him. He became the authority figure many kids did not have at home. He provided structure, discipline, and guidance to all of us. Every day. Without fail.

Marching band took a toll on my knees. I eventually tore a tendon on my left knee and needed surgery to repair it. I was incredibly nervous while being prepped by the nurses before my operation. The smells, the sounds, the IV being inserted, the anesthesiologist asking questions. The nurse took out a marker and drew the letter X on my knee and asked why she did that.

She answered, "It's to let the doctor know what knee to operate on". *What knee to operate on? What? That is the wrong knee!* The medication flowing through the IV started taking hold and I was drifting off. "That's the wrong kn...." I mumbled.

Upon waking from my delightful slumber, the X on my knee drifted into my consciousness. "Wait! Just Wait! Please, did they do the correct knee? Nurse. Which knee??!!"

The nurse giggled and said, "Of course they did the correct knee. Relax and take your pain meds."

I whispered out loud thinking it was too myself, "Thank you sweet baby Jesus." I looked over and saw my mother sitting next to me.

"Thank you for what?" she asked.

I blurted out the mishap with the marker and the X, and she said, "What!? I can't believe that!"

It felt good to see that she cared about the potential mishap and what could have happened to me. She shrieked, "That was so dumb of you! You should have let them operate on the other knee, and we could have sued them for lots of money! God, you're so stupid."

I allowed myself to give into the rush of the recently administered pain medication. The medication that lulled me back into a state of no pain.

***

Soon, love entered my life again. Dan was my first love. He was a blond-haired, green-eyed sophomore. He played second-base for the Junior Varsity baseball team and had a suave and smooth way about him. He was good-looking and he knew it. I was head- over-heels instantaneously, and I could not believe he was interested in me - an insecure, desperate-for-love freshman. Our relationship took off and we became serious fast. The months flew by, and he growingly became inpatient to have sex. I was a very inexperienced virgin, and I would not be his first sexual encounter; I eventually agreed, afraid to lose him, afraid to lose my lifeline.

Weeks passed and my period was late. The fear and panic gripped me in a way that it felt like my lungs could not fill up with air. I asked Dan to get a pregnancy test as I could not find the courage to do this myself. We sat on the floor side-by-side holding hands, leaning against the bathroom cabinet anxiously waiting the minutes it took for the stick to reveal my fate. The second hand on his watch ticked by with such fatigue that my heartbeats exceeded the speed of each ticking second.

We stood and stared at the stick for what seemed like an eternity... Then there it is, I was pregnant.

My knees began to quiver, and the blood rushed from my head down to my lower extremities. Dan spun around and took me in his arms and whispered that everything would be okay. I wanted to believe him, but I knew it would be far from okay once my mother found out. I looked deep into his tear-filled eyes and told him she could never know. She would make me terminate the pregnancy and I would never be allowed to see him again. He agreed and we headed to his house to tell his mother. On that 45-minute drive a plan was formulated: get married and have me move into his parents' home with him until we finished high school. We would attend college and buy a sweet modest home close to the water.

Dot was a large-framed woman whose domineering posture and presence overshadowed her prestigious nursing career. We were both terrified telling her as she sat across the dining room table from us. I could see her jaw tighten and her eyes narrow as her glare could see right into my soul.

She took a deep breath and said, "Okay, we will schedule an appointment to confirm the pregnancy, and if confirmed we'll schedule the abortion.

Abortion? I never mentioned an abortion.

My voice was barely audible when I responded, "I don't want an abortion. I want to keep the baby."

Dan's voice, slightly more fervent said, "I agree with Annie.

We want to get married and keep the baby."

Dot stood up and left us at the dining room table. She later came back into the room with her husband, Dan's father. His fists were clenched at his side and his eyes burned with rage. "

"You will not get married, as we will not give our legal consent," he said. His gaze darted to me and said, "And you will get an abortion once the pregnancy is confirmed." They spun around on their heels and left us sitting in utter shock.

The pregnancy was confirmed later that week and the appointment to abort the baby was scheduled. Sitting in second period Spanish class was a good opportunity for me to zone out as I sat in the back of the class. I doodled baby names in my notebook until I decided on one... Brittany. I knew in my heart it was a girl and I knew I could give her more love than any other baby on earth. Even more so, she would love me unconditionally. She would need me, and I would need her. I drew hearts around her name and filled pages of my notebook with the most beautiful name in the world, Brittany.

My report card came home and in the teacher section under comments said, "Annie is a daydreamer. She refuses to focus on class and is currently receiving an 'F'. Please call me with any questions."

I could almost see the hair on the back of my mother's neck raise as she read the teachers comments.

"What on earth can you possibly be thinking about that is more important than paying attention in class?" she seethed. The saliva gathered at the corners of her mouth and soon she would be spitting her hateful words as her temper burned hotter. "You know Annie, you are so stupid. You will never amount to anything in life," she declared. "The way I see it, you are going to marry some low-life gas station clerk and end up barefoot and pregnant, popping out 7 worthless kids and living in a run-down trailer. You'll probably get beaten by your worthless husband and will deserve it too."

Her anger turned to pure joy from the mere thought of that likely future danced through her head. She walked away mumbling… "Barefoot and pregnant, ha!"

I deeply drew in stale air into my deflated lungs and breathed a sigh of relief that went as well as it did. I was not beaten, and I was not grounded from seeing Dan. I would take a beating any day over being grounded from seeing Dan. But one day, I will show her. I will become someone.

***

Laying on that cold table with my feet in stirrups and the doctor prying my knees apart was by far the most humiliating experience of my young life. Dan and his father patiently waited in the waiting room. Dan anxiously fidgeted with his hands while his father browsing through a Fish and Wildlife magazine. Hot tears ran down my face and landed on the paper covered table with a thud.

"Well, I can't feel the baby and if I can't feel it, I can't remove it," said the doctor.

Relief fell over me. Those words were like a lovely melody to my ears. I got dressed and when to the waiting room. Dan leaped from his chair and took me into his strong arms. I whispered into his ear, "Brittany is still alive. He didn't take her from us."

He looked deep into my eyes with shock and disbelief and told me everything would be okay. The nurse summoned us over and rescheduled another appointment in three weeks.

Dan's father, agitatedly mumbled, "Great, now I need to take another day off work to drag you two back up here in three weeks."

I did not care. I still had my baby girl safely tucked away in my tummy.

Three weeks were three more weeks to bond with Brittany and daydream about her little fingers and little toes. Would she have my eyes and his nose? Regardless, she would be perfect. My perfect little girl. Back on that cold, sterile table, the doctor said, "Just like before. Relax and it will be over soon." The pain was electric. My toes curled and I grabbed the sides of the table.

"Nope. Still too small to take. If I cannot feel the fetus next appointment, you will have to go through with the pregnancy, as it will be illegal at that point."

God must want me to have this baby, I whispered. What a blessing this baby will be. Another appointment scheduled for three more weeks.

I left there knowing I would be a mother in roughly 7 months. I laid in the back seat the whole car-ride home watching the beautiful white clouds dance in the crystal blue sky. The smile, not on my face, but within my heart was beaming. Dan turned around from the front seat to give me a look of encouragement. His eyes told me we would be fine; she would be fine. My thoughts soon went to my mother and how proud I was of myself for being able to keep this secret. Just three more weeks and Dan and I would run away with our baby girl to start a new life. A life without threats, fear, and intimidation. A life of love.

"Okay Annie, I can feel the baby this time," the doctor exclaimed. "Here we go."

I have never felt such searing pain in my life. The sounds of the machines, the lights in my eyes, the removal of the one unconditional love I would ever experience: taken from me. I screamed the guttural scream of an animal. The nurse holding me down and I tried to escape the jaws of death.

"Please, please don't take her!"

The doctor stood back and said, "We are done. Excellent job Annie. See the nurse on the way out for resources to help you recover."

Recover? I would never recover. What did I do? How could I let this happen? Why didn't anyone help me? How can I ever live with this?

I walked into the waiting room and a smile came across Dan's father's face. Dan's head dropped into his hands, and he wept. Dan's father graciously allowed me to come back to their home for a few hours before I was to be taken back to my mother.

He said, "We have a dinner party tonight. You can stay if you can act normal and not cry."

I agreed as I could not hide this kind of pain from my mother. I sat at the dining room table in total dissociation. I could not feel. I could not think. I could not make out what people were saying. I choked down my food and asked to be excused. I went to the bathroom and threw up. I slipped into Dan's bedroom and called my best friend, Tina. Tina cried when I told her Brittany was gone. I begged her to ask her mom if I could spend the night as I could not go home and face my mother.

"Hold on," Tina said, "I will ask her." The line went quiet as I anxiously waited.

Finally, she said "She said yes. Come over. Everything will be all right Annie."

Dan's father dropped me off at Tina's house later that evening and as I walked through the front door, I was embraced by my best friend.

She had a terrified look on her face as she said, "My Mom needs to talk to you. I had to tell her what was going on with you."

The vail of fear flowed over my body and I felt light-headed.

"Annie, Tina told me what you did, and you need to go home. You will never be able to see Tina again as she will not be allowed to associate with a murderer."

I could hear Tina weeping in her bedroom.

"I'm sorry Mrs. Reed. I did not want to lose my baby," I whispered.

"Annie, you did not lose it, you killed it."

Ms. Reed dropped me off in front of my home. I could see the lights on inside, so I knew my mother was home and awake. I swallowed the lump stuck in my throat and walked in through the front door.

"Annie, is that you? I thought you were staying the night at Tina's house."

"Yes mom. I have my period with awful cramps so I'm going straight to bed."

I heard her get out of bed and make her way to her bedroom door. I hurried towards my bedroom and almost made it when I heard, "Annie! What is wrong with you?" My mother was a bloodhound with a sixth sense.

"I told you, bad cramps."

Said further probed, "Why are your eyes red? What were you doing at Tina's?"

Oh God. What if she called Tina's mom to ask if something was going on? What if Tina's mom told her?

"Mom, it's so painful I was crying. I just want to take Tylenol and get into bed with my heating pad."

The seconds ticked by like hours while she was processing my words and formulating a conclusion. "Okay. See you tomorrow," she mumbled as she turned around to go back to bed.

I fell into bed, same clothes on, as the waterbed sloshed around from my fall. The waves felt like I was laying on a raft in the middle of the turbulent Atlantic Ocean. I wish I were floating out in the ocean, I thought. I wish the water would swallow me whole and reunite me with Brittany. I am a murderer. How could I ever look at a mirror again? How could I endure this pain? I have lost my daughter, my best friend, and my self-dignity all in one day. I let the waves lull me to sleep. A sleep so deep, so dark, and so lonely.

The next few days, Dan seemed distant. He was not returning my phone calls and he was reserved with me in the hallways at school. Did he hate me because I killed his daughter? Did he hate me as much as I hated myself?

I was in my usual daydreaming state in Spanish class when Jennifer leaned over and whispered, "Are you still with Dan? I heard he was out on a date with Michelle last night."

"What?" I screamed. The students all turned around and the teacher fell silent.

"Is there something you would like to share with the class, Ms. Williams"?

My eyes darted around the room, "No, Mrs. Ortega, sorry."

I excused myself to use the restroom. Instead, I ran down the hall to Dan's class. I peered through the small window in the door until I got Dan's attention. I motioned for him to come out into the hallway. He reluctantly excused himself from class and met me in the hallway.

"Jennifer just told me you went out on a date with Michelle last night. Is that true?" I knew the answer when his eyes shifted downward, and he shuffled his feet.

"How could you?" I bellowed.

Dan grabbed me by the shoulders and said, "I just can't deal with all this drama anymore. I want a normal life. I want to be with someone else."

I could not believe what my ears heard. "Drama?" I exclaimed. "You think I wanted this. We were supposed to be married. Have a life together. Love each other till the end of time."

"I'm sorry Annie. I do love you. I just can't…"

I turned and ran down the hallway. I hid in the bathroom stall until school was over and took the bus home. The pain was too much. The loss was too overwhelming. The grief was swallowing me whole.

I got into the house, threw my backpack onto the bed and headed to the medicine cabinet. I heard of other girls cutting their wrists or taking a bottle of Tylenol to kill themselves, but I did not know anyone who actually did this. I grabbed the full bottle of Tylenol out of the cabinet and dumped the pills into the palm of my hand. How many pills does it take to kill yourself? I cannot mess this up, I thought to myself. I will just take the whole bottle. My mouth was so dry despite gulping them down, 4-5 pills at a time with water. They tasted horrible as they stuck to the back of my throat. When my palm was empty, I sat down and leaned against the bathroom cabinets. The same spot where Dan and I sat waiting for the pregnancy test results. *'I wish I could go back in time.'* I thought. I would have just run away. It is too late now. What's done is done.

At that moment, I felt a warm sensation flow though my body and a voice telling me to get up. I looked around but no one was there. Was it God? It could not be because God surely does not love me anymore. Before I knew it, I was on my feet running downstairs and knocking on the neighbor's door, Mr. and Mrs. Shoemaker. The couple had been living in that apartment for many years and I would help them carry groceries inside when needed. Mr. Shoemaker was 82 years old and recovering from knee surgery. He answered the door, and a warm smile came over his face.

"Mr. Shoemaker, I swallowed a bottle of pills, and I don't know what to do. I don't want to die." Mr. Shoemaker called 911 and just then, my mother pulled into the parking lot, just getting home from work.

My heart sank and my breathing became labored. "Mr. Shoemaker, my mom is going to be so mad at me." My heart was pounding so hard, I could feel it pulsating in my ears. He looked worriedly at my mother as she was approaching the door.

"Annie, what is going on?" my mother questioned.

"Ms. Williams, Annie has overdosed, and the paramedics are on their way."

My mother was so good at putting on an act of caring if it is in front of others. "Oh Annie, my sweet love. It is going to be okay."

The paramedics put me into a hospital bed while the ER doctor told me to swallow this black liquid. "It's going to taste awful, but drink it all down Annie," he sternly demanded.

I did as I was told and soon began to heave and vomit.

Between gasps, I asked why I was throwing up.

"To save your life Annie," the nurse gently said.

It seemed like hours I was vomiting up black tar. I was thoroughly exhausted as my stomach quieted and my head hit the pillow. I looked over and my mother was sitting there in the chair beside the hospital bed.

"Are you better now?" she asked. Am I better? I had no idea what I felt. "You know, Mr. Shoemaker was very shaken up. Why would you put that poor man through that? What is he going to think of us? Of me?" she quizzed. "Poor man, poor, poor man."

I truly hated her at that moment. I wanted nothing more than to feel arms around me and to be told I was loved, and all would be well.

The involuntary hold was signed, and I was off to the psych ward for 72 hours. I begged, I pleaded not to go, but the doctor said I had no choice. The police drove me to the unit across town and as we pulled up to the front door, two men in scrubs came to meet the police officers. The officer exited the car and started talking and laughing with the two men.

I pressed my ear against the car window but could not make out what was said. I imagined it was something like, "Stupid teenager trying to kill herself and get attention."

I felt a burning hatred for those three men. How could they laugh at a time I was in so much pain? The two men escorted me in through three locked doors. I sat in a tiny, cold room with no windows and no pictures on the walls.

A therapist sat in a chair with a desk chained to the wall. "So, Annie. Tell me what brought you here today?"

What brought me here? What brought me here is years of abuse at the hands of an untreated Bipolar, Borderline Personality Disorder mother with rage issues and narcissistic traits. A mother that was sober for 6 years but did not follow a program. A best friend that was forced to defriend me, a boyfriend that left me for another girl, and a baby that was torn from my body.

I could not find those words, so I responded, "Nothing. Whatever." I was sure not going to spill my guts to a stupid therapist who does not care anyway.

"I see by the paperwork, you took a bunch of pills to kill yourself," he so studiously announced.

"No shit Sherlock," I snarkily responded.

"Well," he said, "You will have a few days in the unit to think about it."

And with that, I entered a large, outdated room with a TV blaring and patients wondering around in circles along the perimeter of the room. Some were sitting in the corners, legs bent up against their chest, hugging their knees and rocking back and forth. The two large plastic couches were stained and starting to tear. The air was heavy and smelled like medicine and wet socks.

"Annie, come with me. I will show you your room."

I followed the nurse past the woman growling and grabbing at dust particles in the air. The room was small with two beds separated by a small table bolted to the floor. The bed had a plastic mattress, plastic pillow with a fitted sheet and pillowcase. An orange torn blanket was neatly folded and sat at the bottom of each bed.

"Annie, this is your bed. Lights turn off at 9pm, and you will lay here quietly if you cannot sleep. As you see, there is no door, so we will be checking on you every 30 minutes throughout the night. You will make the bed in the morning after being woken at 6am sharp. You will be expected to attend all groups and participate appropriately. Any questions?"

Yeah, when the hell do I get out of this shithole?

"No ma'am," I mumbled.

"Good. It is almost group time, then bedtime. The psychiatrist will see you in the morning." *Great*, I thought to myself. Another 'professional' to assume what is wrong with me.

The two techs on the unit divided us into groups and the female patients were assigned to the female tech and the male tech to the males.

"When I call your name, grab a clean pair of scrubs and follow me."

It was shower time, and we each had 5 minutes to shower, dry off and get dressed. My name was called, and I reluctantly got off the couch in the common area. The bathroom consisted of one room with a toilet, sink, shower, and was freezing cold. The shower was sectioned off by a half wall, no shower curtain.

"Undress and get under the running water", she barked.

"Can you leave first please?" I questioned.

"No can do. I have to stand here and watch you undress and shower."

What? There is no way I am going to do this. She saw my apprehension and became more annoyed.

"I couldn't give a shit what you want. Time's a ticking. You've got 4 minutes left. You can remove your clothes, or we will do it for you."

I stripped down, trying to conceal myself as best as I could and stepped under the cold water. I shook so hard it was difficult to lather my hair and hold onto the tiny bar of soap. Finally, I wrapped myself in a tattered towel and have never felt more grateful that the experience was almost over with. I dressed, went to my room, snatched the blanket off my bed and headed to the couch to tuck myself as deeply into the corner of it as possible that no one could ever find me.

The group talked about alcohol use and abuse. I thought, *why was I having to sit through this. I don't drink much.* Bedtime finally arrived and I crawled into the uncomfortable, plastic bed and wrapped myself in the orange blanket as it felt like a meat locker on that unit. My roommate was in her 40's with matted hair, terrible body odor, and long, dirty fingernails. She laid facing me, mumbling to herself. *I had to get out of here,* I thought to myself. These people are crazy. I'm not crazy. I'm just sad and misunderstood. I tried so hard not to close my eyes and fall asleep. I needed to keep an eye on that crazy lady staring at me. Was she plotting my death? As I lay there trying to make sense of her and things in general, I drifted off to sleep.

***

The heat of her foul breath on my face was revolting. I slowly came out of slumber, opened my eyes to see my roommate leaning

over me, nose to nose and mumbling how she hated the color blue. I jerked my body back so quickly, my head hit the side of the wall. I let out a whale and leaped out of bed.

The nurse came running it and screamed, "Shut up! You are going to wake up the whole damn unit."

I choked back tears and said, "She was in my face. I cannot sleep in here. Please, I am begging you, let me out of here."

She snickered and said, "Honey, that's not up to me. My job is to keep you quiet. If you cannot, I will get an order for medication to make sure you are quiet."

I crawled back into bed, and the nurse allowed my roommate to pace the common area. I laid there thinking of Brutus, my faithful companion. I know he is out there somewhere, maybe thinking of me. I hugged my pillow tight and fell off into a deep sleep.

What seemed to be the longest night of my life ended at daybreak when I heard screams coming from the common area. I looked over at my roommate's bed, and it was empty. I crept out of bed and peered out to observe the commotion. My roommate had her fingers clasped tightly around the unit nurse's strands of blond hair while yanking her backwards towards the bare floor. The nurse let out a screech as she struggled to untangle her hair from the patient's grasp. She reached up and grabbed hold of their thumbs, pulling violently in an attempt to free herself. My roommate yelped in pain and released the grasp on her hair. The unit techs then quickly rushed in and took down my roommate in a well-orchestrated, gentle yet assertive manner.

I crawled back into bed and pulled the foul-smelling blanket back up to my chin and curled up into a tight ball. Moments later, the unit psychiatrist came into my room and shouted, "What are you still doing in bed? Get up and talk to me". He stood 6 feet tall, thin and slightly hunched over. His reading glasses clung to the end of his crooked nose, and he reeked of cigarette smoke. He stood in my doorway until I was out of bed and slipped into my shower shoes. I reluctantly followed him across the unit and into his tiny makeshift office at the corner of the day area. The second unit nurse was already present in the office shifting through paperwork in my chart.

"Annie, take a seat and tell me why you are here," he almost said with a sigh.

Why am I here? He knows damn well why I am here. It's written right there in my chart. I felt it be best not to verbalize those thoughts directly as I wanted out of that horrid jail immediately. I had heard if the psychiatrist thought you were no longer a threat to yourself or someone else, he had the power to let you out before the 72-hour hold was up.

"Doctor, I took a bunch of pills because I was sad and not thinking clearly," I almost whispered as the shame and guilt bubbled up to my voice box.

"Why did you do that?"

What a good question. I do not know. I hated my mother. I hated what Dan did to me. I hated I killed my baby. I hated my life. I had no hope. I had no coping skills. Pick your poison, doctor.

"I don't know," I mumbled. How can I put into words all those thought and feelings?

"Well, Annie, we will give you another day here to think about it."

Wait, what?! Another day? No way! "Please doctor! I have to get out of here! I swear, I will not ever do that again. My roommate will kill me, please!!"

He stayed focused on writing in my chart as his glasses almost slid off his nose. I turned to the nurse, "Please," I mumbled.

"Have a wonderful day, Annie. I will see you again the morning. I expect to see you in the common area bright and early." I sat in shock and disbelief. I felt frozen to my seat while they sat blankly staring at me. "Goodbye Annie."

With that, I made my way back to my bed, but was stopped halfway there by the unit tech stating, "Oh no. You are not allowed to be in bed until it is bedtime. You will remain in the common area and attend all group sessions. After your first group session, we will serve breakfast."

This day keeps getting better and better. The sessions were long and boring, and I could not relate at all. They were focused on alcohol abuse and treatment, life skills, and education on how to be medication compliant. Every hour, patients were let outside into a caged patio for cigarette breaks. I did not bring cigarettes with me, but a few patients were happy to share theirs with me. Compared to the occasional skinny Capri Lights I would smoke with my friends; the smokes were disgustingly foul. However, the urge to step outside and bask in the sunlight made up for the terrible taste in my mouth.

For some reason I was moved to a different room for sleep that night. My roommate was a very timid young female. I tried to initiate a conversation, but she stayed silent with her eyes fixated on the corner of the ceiling. I was so extremely grateful to have her as a roommate and felt I would have a good night's sleep. I was woken numerous times during that night by random screams coming from other rooms, and the frigid cold temperate that unit was set too. I laid there rehearsing what I would say to the doctor in the morning. It had to be convincing. *How do you fool a psychiatrist??* I woke to voices right outside my door and realized it was morning. I jumped out of bed hoping I would be in the common area before the psychiatrist started his rounds; I was successful.

I saw him slip on his medical coat as he entered the unit and headed towards his office. My name was finally called, and I was ushered to his office where he was waiting with the same nurse.

"So, Annie. How are you feeling today?"

How the f*ck do you think I am feeling jackass?

"Much better doctor, thank you." I had to learn the art of deception early in life to avoid negative and punitive consequences inflicted by my mother. Smile through the pain and mask your true feelings as all costs.

"What has changed to make you feel better?" he asked, his eyes and attention fixed on my expression and body language.

"Well, I have given it a lot of thought and I realize I have a lot to live for. I want to finish school and eventually go to college," I said brightly. I thought, *Okay Annie, do not lay it on too thick. He will see right through it.*

"Wow. What a great turn around just since yesterday, Annie."

Oh man; is that sarcasm or is he being genuine? I am screwed.

"Thank you doctor. If I ever thought of hurting myself again, I will reach out to someone first," readjusting my tone to a flatter, yet compliant stance.

After numerous more questions, he said with a tinge of annoyance, "Okay Annie. We will let you out today. We will call your mother to let her know. Once all the paperwork is done, we will let you know."

It worked! I fooled them! I was getting out of one hell hole to go back to another.

I was not released until late afternoon as apparently it takes 7 hours to complete paperwork. My mother was waiting for me in the lobby as I exited through a series of locked unit doors.

She saw the nurse ushering me out and said, "Oh Annie. I'm so glad to see you. Let's go home."

I thought, *sure, you are. Cannot wait to see the real emotions once we are alone in the car.* I could not wait to get into my shower and wash off the stink of that awful place off my body and out of my hair. The car ride home was quiet for which I was grateful for. After a 30-minute shower, I slipped into my favorite baggy sweats and climbed into bed.

My mother quietly slipped into my room, "Annie, I want to talk to you."

Are you kidding me?

"Mom, I'm so tired. Please, just leave me alone. I don't want to talk."

I knew my words could lead to an explosive outburst and physical punishment, but at that point I did not care. I was so beaten down and depressed that she could have killed me, and I would not have cared.

"Okay Annie. We will talk in the morning."

I slowly and rhythmically rocked myself to sleep in my soothing waterbed. I dreamed of Brutus and running through the fields with Ralphie tucked tightly in my arms. One day I will run so far, I will soar.

Chapter Seven

"It is during our darkest moments that we must focus to see the light."
~ ***Aristotle***

Jules, my best friend, and I frequently worked evenings together at Maria's ice cream shop. Jules was blonde, with beautiful blue eyes. She was smart, way smarter than me, but lacked logic. I loved her and confided in her often. The store phone on the wall rang while I was with a customer, so Jules answered it.

She listened for a minute, and said, "Annie, it's your dad."

What? Why would he call me at work? She took over for me and I picked up the phone.

"Hi, dad. You okay?" He was crying and his speech was rapid.

"Annie, I just opened the mail and received a hospital bill for services rendered to you a few weeks ago. You tried to kill yourself?" he shouted. "What the hell is going on down there? Do I need to come get you and bring you back to Indiana?"

I whispered, "No dad. I am fine. Really, I am okay."

But that was the furthest thing from the truth. I was not okay. I will never be okay. I am in total survival mode and do not need anyone's help.

"I love you, dad. I'll call you later."

With that, I hung up the phone and returned to scooping ice cream. It was ten minutes before closing time, so Jules and I started our nightly closing process. The shop was empty of customers.

"Jules, fill the mop bucket with water, and I will wipe down all the tables."

Jules swung the large faucet arm over to the edge of the sink and began filling the huge yellow bucket that sat on the floor. She came out and helped me finish wiping tables and chairs. We laughed and squirted each other with our spray bottles. It felt so good to laugh with Jules. We both looked down at the floor at the same time and saw the water pooling around our feet.

"Jules! Did you leave the water running in the stock room?!" We both ran back to the stockroom, slipping and sliding across the wet tile floor.

"Jules, lock the front door and I'll start mopping this up." Jules skidded across the shop, locked the door and we both mopped up as quickly as possible. Just then, we heard a loud knock on the glass of the locked front door. I approached the door and saw the owner and another man I did not recognize. I could see the anger blazing in the owner's eyes as I unlocked the door.

"Annie, why is the door locked three minutes before closing?" he questioned.

"Mr. Adams, we accidently flooded the floor filling the mop bucket, so I locked the door so no customers would enter, slip and fall on the wet tile floors."

Mr. Adams looked over at the other man, then back at me. "Well Annie, this is Mr. Condan." I extended my hand out to shake, but he did not reciprocate.

"Mr. Condan here is interested in purchasing the shop but would not think too kindly of employees closing a store early and losing business. So as a result, you are fired."

Fired?

"But Mr. Adams, I was thinking the safety of customers was more important than keeping the store open for only three more minutes."

"Well Annie, you thought wrong." Jules began to cry as I gathered my few belongings and exited the store.

The cool air felt so good on my skin as I walked through the parking lot to my car. I breathed it deeply into my lungs until I felt lightheaded. I thought of Brutus, I thought of Indiana, I thought of the click-click, click-click of the train on the tracks those mid- summer nights. What if my dad was right? What if I moved back to Indiana, found Brutus, and finished my high school years there? I could pack my car with only the things I needed and make the 1,500-mile drive by myself. My mind swirled with the possibility. I laid in bed that night and formulated a plan. I would drive home right after school tomorrow, pack my car, and leave before my mother returned home from work. I could tell her I work after school, so she would not even expect me home until 10pm. I could reach the Georgia line before she would even realize I was gone. It took hours before sleep found me. The plan was in place. My dad would be so surprised.

Morning came and I was full of anticipation. I grabbed a banana and headed out the door to school.

"Bye mom. I work tonight after school, so I won't be home until 10:15pm."

My eyes met hers, and for a brief moment I thought I would miss her. I thought of how much this will hurt her. I thought this was the last moment I would ever see her again.

"Good-bye mother. Have a nice…day."

That day dragged by like molasses. The minutes felt like hours. Finally, the seventh period bell rang, and I ran out of the school into the parking lot. I started the car and prayed it would carry me safely on my 1,500-mile journey. I got home, grabbed as much of what would fit in my car and counted the money I had stashed in my secret hiding place - $76.15. I was confident I could make it with that. I would sleep in my car if I needed to but would try to drive straight through. I used the bathroom, filled a small cooler with drinks and snacks and headed for the front door. I opened it, stood on the threshold, and said good-bye.

I ran down the cement stairs to the parking lot and saw the hood of my car open. The rear faced the condo, so I could not see if someone were standing at the front of my car looking at the engine. Why is my hood open? I slowly reached the trunk, set my cooler down and approached the front of the car. There I found my mother in her work clothes pulling the last spark plug out of my engine.

"There," she exclaimed. "That should do it!"

My mouth fell open as she juggled the spark plugs in her hand like a set of brass balls.

"Where do you think you're going?" as the corners of her mouth grew to a snicker.

"Nowhere," I mumbled.

"Do you think you are going to leave me? Just take off in this piece of shit car. No good-byes?"

I could not find the words. I wanted to scream and yell. Tell her I hated her. Tell her I hated school. Tell her I hated my life, but I could not. I did not have the courage. She took the spark plugs with her into the house and left me standing at the front of the car. I saw Mr. Shoemaker peering out his kitchen window at me. Our eyes met each other's, and he gave me a wink. Was this a wink letting me know he tipped off my mother, or a wink signifying he understood why I needed to leave? Either way, it did not matter. My time would come.

***

Months passed and I eventually got my spark plugs back. Of course, I did not know how to install them, so I had to use my work earnings to pay a mechanic to place them back into the engine. I was no longer dependent on my friends to give me rides to and from school, thanks to my newfound independence. One step closer to freedom.

I paid to have my own phone line installed in my bedroom. Mom could not stand how often I was on the phone, so demanded I limit calls to 20 minutes or get my own line. I paid for the installation and made the monthly payments. Half my weekly paycheck went into my savings account and the other half paid for my phone, hygiene products, gasoline, clothing, and entertainment. Not much was left for entertainment, but enough for a movie or two and a pack of cigarettes.

I felt especially good that evening. I placed some peel-and- eat shrimp on my plate with cocktail sauce and headed into my bedroom. Jules was supposed to call me soon and I needed to fill her in on what happened in second period today. The phone rang and my hands were dripping in shrimp juice and cocktail sauce. Of course, I forgot a napkin. What to do, what to do?!

"Mom, please get my phone. I can't get it right now!"

She came out from her bedroom and saw me sitting on the bed, by my phone with, fingers messy with food.

Her eyes narrowed as she picked up the phone, "Hi Jules. Hold on."

She set the phone down and like lightning, she knocked the plate of food out on my hand. The shrimp and cocktail sauce hit the wall and slowly slid down to the floor. She pushed me down on the bed, straddled me as her hands firmly pressed down on my shoulders. The movement of the waterbed made it hard to keep her balance.

Her eyes were electric. Her mouth snarling like a rabid dog. "Don't you ever talk to me that way! I am not your maid. You answer your own damn phone you ungrateful bitch!"

At that moment, I felt something snap inside of me. I could no longer stay silent. The emotions, the anger, the frustration coursed through my blood like adrenaline. With one surge of motion, I flipped her off me and crawled on top of her. I straddled her as she kicked and punched at me. My shrimp-soaked hands found her neck and I squeezed down tightly. My grip was fueled with years of rage, misunderstanding, pain, and fear. I lowered my upper body until my nose was millimeters from hers. She clinched her fists and pounded on the sides of my torso in efforts to loosen my grip around her shrinking neck.

"If you ever touch me again. If you ever scream at me again. If you ever look cross-eyed at me again, I will kill you." I shrieked, my voice trembling but firm.

Her eyes bulged and her lips started turning blue. My body shook violently as the rage flowed through me. She tried to speak but my hands could not loosen their grip. It was as if my hands had a life of their own and I had no control over them.

"Do you understand me? Never again!"

She mouthed the word 'Yes' as her fists hitting my ribs had less force behind them at this point.

I looked deep into her hazel eyes and saw fear. No anger, no rage, just pure fear. Probably the same fear she saw so many times in my eyes over the years. Her eyes begged me to stop, to let her go, to let her live. Just like my eyes so many times over the years. My grip loosened and I slumped over her with my head resting on her chest. We both gasped for air and too weak to move. I flopped over onto the bed beside her, and we both looked up at the ceiling watching the fan blades gently glide through the air, cooling our skin. In that moment, we were equal. She no longer controlled me. She no longer intimidated me. She no longer had me. I was my own being, with my own voice, with my own destiny. She slowly sat up and exited the room.

I could faintly hear Jules yelling over the phone, "Annie! Annie! What is going on?!"

I picked up the phone and said, "I'm okay." And this time, it was true.

***

My alcohol intake increased, and as it did, I became more reckless. I surrounded myself with friends that liked to drink as well. Fred worked at the local grocery store and would place a case of Bartel's and James wine coolers right outside the receiving dock out back. We would pick it up and head to the local strip mall and wait for Fred to get off work. All the high school kids met at this mall in the parking lot to plan where to party. The destination would usually be way out in the woods around Stagecoach Pond at the powerlines. Everyone would bring their own booze, cigarettes, and subwoofers.

We always built a bonfire and back the pickup truck around it and sit or dance in the beds. A fight would eventually break out, and it was always settled with fists. Couples would walk off deeper into the woods and have sex.

On the rare occasion, the cops would show up, make us dump out the alcohol and shoo us out of there. There were no calling parents, no arrests made, no concerns about drunk driving. Just get the hell out and do not come back. Sometimes it would take a while to actually leave, a few friends would occupy the cops, as another would frantically run around searching for the semi-conscious friend or two passed out in a nearby field. The least drunk person would be the one to slip behind the wheel and take each one of us home.

One particular night on the drive home, I sat in the backseat and bounced around, belting out lyrics to The Violent Femmes with two friends. How cool would it be to open the car door as we were speeding down I75, lean out and get my face as close to the painted traffic lines painted on the road as they whizzed by? I decided to give it a try.

I grabbed ahold of my friend with my left hand, opened the door, leaned out and held onto the bottom of the doorframe with my right hand. Between the alcohol and the speed by which the painted broken lined sped past my face was dizzying and mesmerizing. What if I just let go of my friends' hand? What if I gave into the thrill and become one with the road? The rushing wind stole my breath, as I inched closer into the road, just inches now from my face.

"Annie!"

The moment was gone as my friend jerked me back into the car, leaned over me and slammed the door closed.

"What the hell are you doing?" she screamed as she took my face in her hands. We both burst out laughing and continued butchering the lyrics to 'Cheeseburger in Paradise' by Jimmy Buffet.

By the grace of God, I never hung out with people who took hard drugs. In my small southern town, full of wealth and affluence, drugs were rampant and at your disposal whenever you wanted them. I was offered pills on occasion, but never took anything. Years back, an officer came to our middle school and talked about the dangers of drugs.

He stated some drugs can kill you instantly, even with the very first dose. This statement lodged in my brain and carried me through my teen years. To this day, I am so incredibly grateful this stuck with me, as I would have definitely overdosed or killed myself if I got hooked on drugs. Alcohol was my drug of choice, and thankfully I had friends that watched over and cared for me when I could not care for myself.

Chapter Eight

"Life is a succession of lessons which must be lived to be understood."
~ ***Ralph Waldo Emerson***

That old '72 Chevy Chevette broke down every other day at this point which would leave me stranded on the side of the road at the most inopportune times. I would pull off into the wide, grassy median in efforts for higher visibility. I stood outside the car in the hot, blazing summer sun and wait, wait, wait. No cellphone, no mechanic skills, just waiting for the mercy of a friend; not a stranger. Periodically, a man would pull over and ask if I needed help.

I would flash a smile and reply, "Nope. Just waiting for my friend."

Eventually, a high school buddy would inevitably pull up behind me and offer a ride. "Again Annie? Get in!"

Getting into the cool car after standing out in the hot Florida sun was heaven.

"I soooo need a different car," I would exclaim, "but saving my bucks for something special."

One day, I would buy a plane ticket to Indiana and escape.

Leave the car, my mother, and the past behind.

James was the next man to enter my mother's life. He was creepy to me, but he made my mother happy which kept her focus off me. She had a man, was happy, so now was the time. I waited for the exact moment I thought would afford me the best outcome for my plea. I took her hands into mine and looked deep into her eyes.

"Mom, please let me go. Let me live with my father. You have James, and he will make you happy. I need to find my own happiness."

I think she felt my desperation in that moment. I think she knew she could not hold me back any longer. Our time was up.

"Go. If you think he will love you more than me, you are wrong," she snapped back sharply. "Don't you remember how he touched you inappropriately? Don't you remember how he raped you as a baby? That's why I divorced him when you were barely two years old."

She was desperate, pacing, ringing her hands, and walking circles around the dining room table, grasping at straws. "I sacrificed my financial stability of being married for you. To protect you, and this is how you pay me back? Run back to your abuser. You were made for each other." How could she continuously hurt me in the most devastating, ephemeral way possible? My stomach seized and my head began to spin.

"What are you talking about?" I exclaimed. "He has never hurt me, touched me inappropriately, or raped me! I would have remembered that! This is your desperate attempt to keep me under your thumb, and it will not work."

She slowed her pace, she composed herself. "Go, you stupid, selfish girl. I will help you pack.

I was about to be free. I was about to start my new life in my old town. I would enter high school there and complete me senior year. I would make new friends, reconnect with old friends, and heal. The excitement breathed fresh air into my aching body. I called all my friends to say good-bye. I spent the next two days on the sandy white beaches soaking up the sun and playing beach volleyball with friends. Within a few days, I would be on a plane heading for freedom.

I sold that old, beat-up car for $200 and thought I made out like a bandit. I crammed the cash deep into my jeans pocket and bid that car farewell. Once in Indiana, I would use my savings to buy another car. That little voice kept popping up at the most unexpected moments over the next couple days, "He raped you. That's why we divorced."

I would quickly dismiss it, but it kept creeping back in. I had to talk with my father about this. I need to give him a chance to explain. I need to do this before I step onto that plane. My hands were shaking when I dialed his phone number. How do I ask such a question? What will his response be? How would I respond? What if it was true?

I slammed the phone down, "I don't want to know. I can live without knowing. I just need to go," I whispered to myself. A couple deep breathes, and I picked up the phone as if it was an involuntary movement. I dialed the number and tears filled my eyes.

"Dad, it's Annie." He sounded so happy, so excited. "I can't wait to see you, Annie. You ready to come here?" he asked.

"Dad, I have an especially important question to ask you and I need you to be totally honest with me. No matter what, just tell me the truth. I will love you regardless of your answer," I pleaded.

"Of course, Annie. You can ask me anything." he responded. Out spilled the whole conversation with my mother. The words were coming out of my mouth more quickly than my lips could move. If I said it really fast, maybe it would hurt less, and we could move on quicker. I finished and the silence was deafening.

"Dad? Are you still there?"

"Yes Annie," he said, "I'm still here." He covered the mouthpiece, but I could still hear the words he spoke to himself. "That bitch. I am going to kill her. Jesus, please help me." He uncovered the mouthpiece and began to cry. "Annie, I love you more than my own life. I would never touch you or hurt you; I swear. Please believe me."

His words were the most sincere, honest words I had ever heard in my life. I knew the truth without a shadow of a doubt. Tomorrow, I would get on the plane.

She drove me to the airport with James in the passenger seat, and me in the back seat. They held hands and giggled about how much fun they were to have in the upcoming weeks. I gazed out the window and watched the trees wiz by creating a green blur through my tears filled eyes. I would see Brutus soon. I just knew I would. Good-bye Florida, good-bye my wonderful friends, good- bye manipulation. They walked me into the airport and up to the gate. I spun around to face her and say good-bye when she asked James to give her a minute with me alone; James agreed.

"Annie, I need to tell you one more thing. It's important you know the whole truth before you go," so sweetly said as she took my hands in hers. "I love you with all my heart. I always have and I always will. You are the light in my life, the air that I breathe. Please come home if you ever change your mind. I will keep your room ready for you."

Her words were so loving, so kind. They were the words I so longed to hear. She gripped my hands a little tighter, and said, "But I in good conscious have to tell you one more thing before you go."

I softly said, "Okay mom."

She looked me deep in the eyes and said, "Your father may not be your real father. He was always drunk and out late at the bars. I got lonely. I needed someone who gave me love. Before I knew it, I was pregnant," she whispered.

She stood frozen waiting for my response. I drew in a deep breath, put my hands on either side of her face, and said, "I love you mom. Have a wonderful life and I wish you much happiness."

I picked up my carry-on bag and headed for the gate. I did not care if he was my father or not. I did not care. He was my father and I loved him. He would always be my father.

I found my seat on the huge 747 airliner. "Yes! A window seat!" I sank into the plush seat, strapped on my seat belt, and pulled the Walkman out of my backpack. I peered out the window as I watched the airline crew get ready to take flight. Their bright orange vests and headsets made them look like they could be part of a music group - maybe The Village People? It was hard to tell, but what I did know was that today marked the beginning of my new life.

Mid-flight, I popped my favorite tape into my Walkman and clicked play. How ironic I thought that this song by U2 was lulling me to slumber: *'I want to run, I want to hide. I wanna tear down the walls that hold me inside. I wanna reach out and touch the flame, where the streets have no name, ha, ha, ha. I wanna feel sunlight on my face. I see that dust cloud disappear without a trace. I wanna take shelter from the poison rain. Where the streets have no name, oh, oh.'*

The wheels making contact on the runway jolted me awake and left me momentarily wondering where I was. My U2 tape had reached the end and shut itself off. Just like I had years ago.

I met my father's eyes across the baggage claim area, and they lit up as soon as we made contact. I buried my face into his chest and melted into his protective arms. The heavy smell of Brillo hair cream and vodka filled my senses. Dad was not able to leave the house without taking at least two shots of vodka first. Some nights he would scream out in his sleep and throw himself out of bed as he fought the foreign soldiers during the Battle of Incheon. The Korean War stole my father's sense of peace and in return gave him such deep anxiety and PTSD that he became disabled in his 40's. No amount of alcohol or Parliament cigarettes quite took away the anxious tremors, but it gave him the courage to face society.

He shared, "How's my favorite girlfriend?" as he stroked my hair backs.

"Fine dad. I can't wait to get home."

"That's what I want to hear. I have the crock pot full and waiting for us at home!"

Dinner took place at a vintage gold flecked, cream and yellow dining room table with yellow metal chairs. The table had been pre- set with care and love. We sat across from each other in front of a steaming hot bowl of stew. A slice of wonder bread smeared with a pat of butter sat beside it and a glass of whole milk filled to the top of a green 1960's glass. Exhaustion started to kick in and my eyes were growing heavy. In reaching for my buttered bread, I tipped over the half-full glass of milk. Before the glass had even emptied out onto the table, I was under the table cradling my legs against my chest and my forehead pressed tightly on top of my knees. I waited for the punishment, but it never came. Instead, my father crawled under the table, sat alongside me with his arm wrapped around my shoulders.

Tears flowed down my face, "I'm so sorry. It was an accident."

"I know," he whispered. My eyes met his and his look of love swept over his stunned face.

In two days, I had my first therapy appointment scheduled with my new therapist. His office was just around the corner from our apartment. It was a small red brick home with an American flag on a short pole waiving in the wind. I climbed the few steps to the front door and thought about turning around. The thought turned into action as I begin to head down the steps.

With that, the door opened, "You must be Annie. Come in. I have a chair waiting for you."

His smile was inviting as he held his hand out to shake mine. It took numerous sessions with him before I could even begin to trust him.

Dr. Stanton was patient and kind, as he systematically removed each layer of brick from the wall I spent years erecting. Over the course of the next three sessions, it all came pouring out of me like verbal vomit that spread to every square inch of his warm, inviting office. The relentless verbal, emotional and physical abuse I had gone through for so many years was outlined in great detail. It felt like I peeled off the layers of a toxic onion until I reached the wretched core. His understanding eyes and affirming nods invited me to continue on my path of memories until there was nothing left. We sat in silence for what seemed to be eons. I was exhausted and felt like I fell down a well. He began to talk, and his voice was distant as if I had cotton in my ears. My head felt swollen, and my heart ached. My ears eventually made sense of his words.

"Annie, you did such an excellent job. Thank you for trusting me," he said softly. His eyes met mine as he shifted in his seat, "I have to tell you. I have been a therapist for 34 years, and I have never heard of such systematic and brutal abuse from a patient!"

I wondered what that meant. Was that good or bad? Would I be, okay? He saw the fear in my eyes as he leaned forward in his chair.

"Now, let us come up with a plan" he said with absolute resolve. It took years for me to truly appreciate the power that plan, and its execution had on my life. It was so simple, yet so incredibly difficult. It took five sessions to create and then practice it in his office. It would be another five months before I would have the opportunity to accomplish my goal, and what a day it was.

It was three months from the time I moved into my new home with my father, to the time I started my senior year in high school. Those months were transformative. My day consisted of playing solitaire cross legged on my bed, listening to music, smoking cigarettes, and drinking beer with my dad, attending therapy once a week and learning the city as I drove block to block. If I got lost, I would stop at a pay phone, call my dad, name the cross streets where I was and memorize his directions on how to get back home.

I was proud of the car I bought with my savings from work in Florida the week after I arrived in Portage. It was a beautiful gold 1980 Datsun 280ZX. It was my second choice following a 1979 soft top Jeep Wrangler. I begged my father to allow me to buy it, but he said I would freeze in the winter. I did not care. I told him it was my money, and I would wear two winter coats if necessary. It was a firm 'no'. The Datsun was fast and so low to the ground I felt like I was hugging the pavement as I dared to go as fast as my nerves let me. I reached 94 mph on an almost flat country road one summer afternoon. I knew it was reckless, but I did not care. The adrenaline dulled the depression just enough for me to feel momentary joy.

I got a job a few days after moving in with my father at an ice cream shop. I consistently worked the evening shift and closed the store by myself. I enjoyed working on my own, but it worried my dad.

He always said, "Annie, you are too trusting. There are bad people out there and you need to be more street-smart."

He would always stand on the second-floor balcony overlooking the parking lot waiting for me to arrive after my work shift. I would get out of my car and yell up to him, "Dad! Why do you wait for me every night?! I am not a little kid. I can walk from my car and into our apartment complex without supervision."

He would always giggle, and say, "I know Annie. I just love waiting for you".

I finished my shift, locked up and got into my little car to head home. I bet he is waiting out on that balcony again, I thought to myself. I blasted the music on the drive home and was feeling particularly good that evening. I pulled into my usual parking spot and wanted to wait in my car until the song I liked was over. A car sped into the parking spot to my right, and then another on my left. One more then pulled up behind me and I was now blocked in with no escape. In front of me was a grassy hill with a short rock wall. The three men jumped out of their cars, and before I could react, one threw open the driver side car door and reached in grabbing my shirt collar.

I could hear my father in the distance screaming, "I've got a gun. Leave now or I'm gonna blow your head off!"

Within seconds, all three men jumped back in their cars and squealed out of the parking lot. I slammed the driver side door shut and locked all doors. My father ran down to the parking lot and gently tapped on the driver side window.

"Annie, it's okay. They are gone. Get out of the car."

I slowly unlocked the door and slid into my father's arms. "Dad, what if you were not there? What if you weren't waiting for me?"

Sobbing into his soft flannel shirt. "Annie, that's why I wait for you. I will always wait for you."

That summer, Dr. Stanton started me on Prozac. He said it would help the depression and decrease my crying episodes. the tears were a daily event. I felt so unanchored. No friends, no outside activities, no hobbies. Of course, this was a time before computers and cell phones. I bought a pellet gun at the local department store, since I thought it would be fun to shoot at homemade targets.

As I held that gun in my hands, it gave me a sense of power, of importance. I could be feared instead of being fearful. Late afternoons were usually spent sitting in the field behind the apartment, listening to The Cure on my

Walkman, smoking cigarettes or cloves and shooting acorns off the pine trees in the dense field beyond my vantage point. I missed my friends. I missed the beach. I missed Brutus. I had no idea how I would find him or if he was still alive. He was always dancing and rolling around right next to me when I laid in the grass staring up at the blue sky as clouds drifted by. I could almost feel his breath on my hand as he would nudge me to get up and chase him around the yard. Maybe he had a new family with a little girl who chases him and takes him fishing on long hikes. Or maybe he was dancing with the clouds and sleeping with the stars.

The night before my first day of my Senior year was a long and sleepless one. What if no one liked me? What if I couldn't find my classes? What if I absolutely hated it? Night turned to morning and morning turned to finding a parking space in the crowded school parking lot. It is incredible how teens have an innate ability to sniff out new prey. I could almost see the wheels of judgement spinning away in each head as they scanned me up and down. My bright Florida clothes stood out along with my bright gold car. Some walked by and mumbled 'rich bitch' under their breath, while others stopped me and asked where I was from as they giggled at my slight Southern accent.

At lunch, I found a quiet spot in the enormous cafeteria. The senior class had 550 students. Much smaller than the 120 I was used to at my old high school. The building was three stories compared to the small one story back home. "Hi, I'm Nichol. What's your name?" As a petite 5'1, Nichol's punk rocker hairstyle added an additional seven inches to her height with the help of Aqua Net hairspray and teasing. She wore black lip stick and had five piercings in each ear. Her eyes were clear blue, and her smile was genuine. Before the end of the school day, she had written directions to her home, and I was invited to stay the night.

The first snowfall of the winter took place early that year and I felt like a kid in a candy shop again. It was beautiful as it fell from the sky and blanketed the earth. In preparation for my first time driving in the snow, I called Nichol and told her I was heading to her house. Nichol told me not to exceed 30 MPH since I would skid on the slick ice. 30MPH on a highway?! Yeah, right. I jumped in my car and took off for her home 30 minutes away. As promised, at 35 MPH I began to skid and lose control of my car. That lightweight Datsun 280ZX was no match for winter weather. I had no idea how to control a car while sliding across ice. I slid into oncoming traffic and saw cars heading straight for me. I frantically spun the steering wheel to get back to the other side of the road. I found myself spinning in circles down the center of the highway. Suddenly, the tires hit a dry patch and the car reacted as you would expect. The car violently lurched from the center of the highways and flew right into a ditch, landing in between a light pole and tree. I sat there panting heavily and trying to regain my bearings. I broke my finger in the chaos, but the car had nary a scratch on it. At this point, I was halfway to Nichol's house. What to do? Turn around and go home, or finish the drive to her home? To her home I went.

She giggled hearing my experience and gleefully said, "I told you so!"

I faithfully attended my weekly sessions with Dr. Stanton. His patience and compassion were the most powerful medicine I could ever consume.

"Annie, have you ever thought of confronting your mother with the abuse and telling her how it made you feel?"

Without skipping a beat, I responded, "Absolutely. It would be really scary, but I have thought about it a lot."

He smiled, "Well, do you want to set up a plan to do so?"

I shifted uncomfortably in my seat, "Y-yes. I would like that." For the next several months, we carefully crafted, examined, and practiced my strategy for approaching my mother. We discussed what I would say and what results I could expect from carrying out this plan. Finally, I felt prepared to confront her.

In the Spring, I planned a 4-day trip to Florida to visit my mother while I was on break from school. It took three days to work up the courage to initiate this conversation.

I walked into her room as she sat reading on her bed, "Mom, can we talk? I have something important I need to say to you."

She smiled as she looked up from her book, "Of course Annie. Sit down". I sat on the edge of her bed as my heart raced and sat squarely to face my abuser.

"Mom, I have been working hard in therapy and I have learned a lot. I have learned you are an abusive alcoholic that has not been able to change the pattern of abuse you suffered from as a child. You have passed it along to me, and as a result, I have suffered greatly. I know you love me and did the best you could. But I have to tell you, it was not good enough."

Her eyes stayed fixated on me and tears came to her eyes. Her tone grew more intense and agitated. "Annie, I knew this day would come someday, and here we are…"

I cut her off, "Mom, please let me finish." She sat quietly as I recounted the moments of humiliation, terror, sadness, confusion, and despair. I also thanked her for the loving moments, the happy times, and the difficulty she must have faced as a single parent.

"Annie, I remember things differently. I remember the happy times. I remember the immense love I had for you and all we have shared."

I almost felt sorry for her in that moment. I suspected she was well versed in blocking out memories of her egregious behavior and violent outbursts and tucking them away somewhere deep in her mind in efforts to continue with this charade of being a 'good mom'.

She yearned for the love she never received as a child, but she was blind to the little girl in front of her who tried her best to fill that void. I finally saw her true self for the first time. A sad, lost little girl longing for love, but not having the tools to create and sustain a loving, healthy relationship.

She had often said she had as many kids as she could so she would never have to feel unloved ever again but, "That was a mistake. They were never there for me despite all my love and hard work." There would never be enough love. At that moment, I vowed to myself I would break the pattern. I would be a great mom. I would be a great wife, friend, and human being. I will continue with therapy as long as it takes to get the job done.

"Mom, maybe consider going into therapy to work on your issues. It's never too late."

She mulled the thought over, "I am open to that. Maybe."

I still had hope she could be the loving mother I desired. Maybe someday we could have a loving relationship. Maybe.

Chapter Nine

"Be decisive. Right or wrong, make a decision. The road is paved with flat squirrels who couldn't make a decision."

~ ***Unknown***

I never quite fit in my senior year but was so grateful for Nichol and her friendship. I skipped so many days of school and hung out with friends or went to the mall that I just barely graduated. The principal called home one day I skipped and talked to my father about missing so many days of school. My father confronted me about this when I arrived home that day and asked if I skipped again. I never lied to my father as he always treated me with kindness and respect.

"Yes, I skipped school and have skipped many days."

He told me I may not graduate, and that terrified me. I cannot think of anything much worse than needing to repeat your senior year. "Okay dad, I will attend school every day until graduation."

I made every effort to follow the rules and attend school, then eventually graduated.

Nichol and I planned to move to Florida once we graduated and get a small apartment together. And that is just what we did. We both had boyfriends that wanted to come with us. Nichol had been dating her boyfriend for three months, but I was not very fond of the guy I was seeing. I saw the relationship more as a friendship, but he wanted more. Nichol and I got in my car, and the boys took their car and we drove nonstop to south Florida.

My father was not thrilled with the idea, but reluctantly agreed saying, "Annie, you are now an adult, and you can do what you want."

We found a one-bedroom apartment to rent and lied to the leasing manager of the complex that it was just the two of us moving in since it was a two-person limit per bedroom. We all crammed into that tiny apartment, and as expected, things fell apart quickly. The two boys moved back to Indiana within a few weeks and Nichol missed home so badly, she moved soon thereafter. The boy I was seeing, Linel, was extremely possessive and stated if he could not have me, no one would. I was grateful he was moving back to Indiana because he became a scary character.

Life was difficult in that tiny apartment alone. I could not afford a washer and a dryer, and the complex laundromat was too expensive, so I washed all my clothes in the bathtub and hung them around the apartment to dry. I lived off Ramen noodles and peanut butter. The sound of gunshots periodically woke me at night and walking to work was a bit nerve-wracking. My car often broke down, so I needed a job I could walk to. I took a job as a dental assistant with a dentist that I babysat for in the past.

The job was challenging, and the dentist had limited patience with my learning curve.

A friend from my old high school heard I had moved back south and asked if I would want to share an apartment with her. I jumped at the chance and moved in with her immediately. I broke the lease where I was living, and the complex eventually came after me for rent. I told them you cannot get blood from a turnip, so sue me if you want your money. And that is exactly what they did. We reached an agreement before court, and I began paying it off slowly.

Life with Gina was fun. I left the dentist's office and started working at her parent's Italian restaurant and felt like I had become part of her family. They were from Italy and fought constantly in Italian. I could not understand a word they said, but I stayed out of their way. On my way to work one afternoon, I was stuck in traffic at a red light. The man in front of me suddenly jumped out of his car, ran over to my open driver side window, and put a gun to my head.

"Len, what the hell are you doing? I thought you were in Indiana."

His hand holding the gun was shaking and vibrating against my temple.

"Bitch, I told you if I couldn't have you no one could."

I tried reaching for the handle to roll up the window, but I was frozen in place. The light turned green, and cars began honking behind me. Len looked around and saw others looking at him.

"Len, if you shoot me, people will identify you. You need to get back in your car and leave."

His finger curled around the trigger, a drop of sweat sliding down his forehead and onto his shoulder. "This isn't finished. I will track you down," he declared before quickly getting back into his car and speeding away.

It took what seemed like eternity for my brain to come back online, but the honking horns brought me back to reality. I drove to work and told Gina and her parents what just happened. Her father pulled me aside and walked me into the storage cooler.

"You know Annie, I can take care of him. I can make it where he is never found again. The Everglades is a short trip from here, you just say the word and it's done."

I looked into his eyes, and I knew he meant every word. "It's okay, I will handle it. Thank you for your offer," I said sheepishly.

The next day I went to the police and requested to file a restraining order. I was told in efforts to have a restraining order approved, a person must threaten to kill you three times and have a witness each time. The police can then be called, and the perpetrator still must be on the premises in an agitated state.

"Wait, What?" I yelled. "I'll be dead by then, you asshole." They did not care. The system did not care.

Two days later Gina and I were on the couch watching a movie, then suddenly saw headlights pointing into the living room which was very odd as the living room faced a lake with only a grassy area between the apartment and the lake. We ran out the front door, and there was Len, in his car revving the gas, and pointing toward our apartment. He slammed on the gas and just stopped short of crashing into the living room. He backed up and repeated this numerous times.

He rolled down the window and calmly stated, "I now know where you live."

The neighbors came out with the commotion and called the police. Linel left before the police arrived, and a report was made. Since he did not verbally threaten me, this did not count as an 'incident'.

The next morning Gina left for work but came running in the house a few minutes later.

"That bastard spray-painted my car!"

I ran out and saw her white Pontiac spray painted black from front to back and side to side.

"Oh my God," I mumbled to myself. Now, he is messing with someone whose family has connections to the mob. I have no control over what happens to him now. The guilt I felt was immense. I felt trapped. I looked over my shoulder everywhere I went and every move I made. I was a prisoner in my body and the police would not help me.

I decided to move out of Gina's home, as she did not deserve to suffer from his sociopathic behavior, and I could not put her life in jeopardy. I decided to move back north to escape him, rent a little apartment and fly under the radar for a while. He would not be able to find me. I left two days later and drove straight through to my father's apartment. He welcomed me back with open arms and said I was safe now. It felt so good to fall deep into his arm and felt that sense of security.

A week later I moved into my own apartment. A 'luxury' one bedroom apartment overlooking a pond for $330 a month, utilities included. I got a job as a waitress in a popular bar that had a large restaurant attached. I worked every night, 10–12-hour shifts. It was tough work, but I liked it, and I became good at it.

I had a regular customer that would come in twice a week, sit at my table, slap a $100 dollar bill on the table and say, "If you keep my glass full, this will be yours at the end of the night." And you betcha I kept that glass full. In three nights, it practically paid for my monthly rent.

The man across the hall from me was a State Trooper and we became fast friends. He was dating a girl I went to high school with, and we became close friends as well. I told them about Linel, and he said, "Don't you worry. If he finds you here, just tell me. I'll take care of him."

It brought me such a sense of comfort. Life was good. I was young, healthy, making good money at my job, made friends, and spent time with my dad.

I finished my shift at work at 1:00 A.M. that night and bundled up in my winter coat and ran through the parking lot to my car. I was so grateful when the car started as it was bitter cold and starting to snow. I forgot to get gas before work and knew I would not make it home unless I stopped to fill up. I pulled into the gas station, tried to pump gas, but realized I needed to pay first. I cursed the pump and ran inside to pay for gas before pumping. The man behind the counter was preoccupied looking outside into the parking lot. I stood at the counter waiting for him to bring his attention back to me. He walked out from behind the counter, passed where I was standing and locked me in the store.

I yelled, "What are you doing?! Unlock the door and let me out!" He picked up the phone and called the police. Why is he calling the police? I need to be the one calling the police! Well, at least someone is calling the police.

He hung up the phone, and calmly said, "A man crawled into your car as you were trying to pump gas. He is lying in your backseat waiting for you to get back in the car". What? That's impossible I would have heard him get into my car.

The police showed up, and I was still trapped inside the gas station. In that moment, I was grateful for being locked in. The officer reached into my backseat and pulled out a man holding a large knife. My knees started shaking and I fell the floor. The man in the store sat on the floor beside me and comforted me. It took an hour to get my bearings and drive home. What if that man did not see him get into my car? What would have happened to me? I laid in bed awake all night and pondered my existence and my purpose on this earth.

I was shaken by the event for a long time, but I decided I wouldn't let it ruin my life. Winter turned to Spring, and I applied for dental hygiene school. My goal was to be a dental hygienist as my experience as a dental assistant prepared me for this career path. I was eventually accepted into the dental hygiene program, and I was over the moon. My first day in the program proved to be eventful.

The professor stated, "This is a rigorous program that requires your full attention."

The program was Monday through Friday 8am to 5pm with daily assignments to be completed at home every evening. I must have looked like a deer in the headlights, because this was not possible. I had to work full time to afford my apartment. And by the way, did I REALLY want to be staring in people's mouths every day for the rest of my life?

I was disappointed at myself for not finding out this information before starting the program. I turned around and walked out of class. I laid in bed that evening and asked myself what I really wanted to do with my life. I want to help people. How could I help people? I could be a therapist. Don't I need to attend a significant amount of schooling for this? *Yes*, I thought to myself. How much do I truly desire this? *A lot*. So, I sought out an advisor and signed up for courses to begin working towards my associate degree. The university was located in Gary, a town known for two things: being the birthplace of The Jackson Five and being on track to become the world's top city for murders. All girls were mandated to have a police escort when leaving class at night. They would walk us to our car and check the backseat before we could get in. We were instructed to run red lights if we felt unsafe in traffic.

I was finally starting to feel more confident that Linel either forgot about me or could not find me. Either way, I was happy to not be looking over my shoulder everywhere I went. I finished three classes at college and stayed remarkably busy working at the bar. My mother would periodically mail letters which were filled with her disappointments in me and how I abandoned her by moving to Indiana. She often promised to pay for my college classes, then would back out days before payment was due. She discouraged me from continuing classes since I was not smart enough to earn a degree, and my life was too full of chaos and drama. "It's so pathetic, Annie. I pray someday you will figure it out and make something of yourself. Chances are you will get pregnant by a loser and end up living in a trailer with twenty kids, destitute and pathetic". The letters always ended with, "I love you so much. Your loving Mother". I would show her. I would become someone. I am someone.

I had a knock on my door but was not expecting anyone. I made it a habit to look through the peephole before unlocking the door. I peered out and my heart leaped to my throat. Len, standing at my door. Pressing his ear against it, listening for movement. I held my breath and stood perfectly still.

How did he find me? I tip-toed over to the phone and called Tom, the state trooper across the hall. Please, answer the phone, please. No answer. Too afraid to leave a message in case Len was able to hear through the door.

"Annie, it's the big bad wolf. I know you are in there. I know what car you drive, and it's out front in the parking lot."

I held my breath and kept watch through the peephole.

"I'm gonna huff, and puff, and blow this door in."

The door was locked, the chain was latched. I needed to trust the safety of the door and not panic. Len eventually got tired of waiting and left. I sat against the door and waited to hear Tom come home. I eventually heard his put his key in his door to unlock it and I cracked mine open.

"Tom. Get in here," I whispered. Tom was just getting off his shift and still dressed in his uniform. I told Tom about Len finding me and knocking on my door.

Tom smiled and said, "I will take care of it."

I was not quite sure what he meant by that, but I did not care.

As long as Len disappeared, I would feel safe.

I decided to change jobs from waitressing to working in a bakery. I worked for a wonderful family that had been in business for 40 years. I primarily worked in the main bakery but would periodically work in a grocery store where the bakery items were sold. They asked me to work a shift at a grocery store bakery that was in a town just south of Chicago, I agreed. The town was run down with many abandoned buildings and residences. It was notorious for daily shootings and murders. I punched in at the time clock in the break room and looked at the fifty or so polaroid pictures thumbtacked to the bulletin board.

A sign stated, *'These people are banned from the store for stealing. If you see one of these people in the store, notify a manager'*. The photos made me a bit uneasy, but I started my shift and began slicing 18 loaves of bread and placed them out on the display table.

A tall, thin man in a long trench coat approached the counter and stated it was his son's third birthday and he wanted a very particular cake. He swayed back and forth and slurred his words. He reeked of body odor and alcohol.

"I want a cake, and I want it now. It has to be blue, purple, eight layers, and not cost more than three bucks."

I started to get uncomfortable as I knew we did not have a cake like that, and I was reluctant to tell him I could not provide it. He fidgeted with items in his trench coat pockets as he tried to right himself and stand straight.

"Well? Give it to me! If you do not give it to me now, I'm gonna blow your freaking head off."

He pulled open his trench coat and exposed a rifle strapped to his side. His eyes grew big as if to emphasize his threat, waiting for my response. Time seemed to slow down, and things moved in slow motion. A crowd was now standing behind him as he grew more agitated and caused a scene.

Why isn't anyone tackling him? There are at least three big men standing in the crowd. I locked eyes with these men as if to plead for their intervention; it did not happen. Okay, I am on my own here and I need to come up with something creative.

"That sounds like an impressive cake!" I exclaimed. "We don't have it here, but I saw the exact same cake you want at the other bakery we have down the street. I will jump in my car and bring it to you. I will even give it to you for free as it is your son's birthday."

My words hung in the air, and his eyes were fixated on me, and he processed what I just said. God, please let him be satisfied with that answer.

Finally, he said, "Okay. I will be back in 10 minutes. If you do not have that damn cake, I'm going to blow holes through you!"

And with that, he spun on his heel and left the store.

To my utter shock and dismay, the crowd that was standing behind him slowly went back about their business as if it was just another day. I grabbed the phone off the wall, slid down to the floor behind the display cases and called the police.

I could barely get the words out, but they assured me they would be on their way. I stayed plastered in that spot on the floor as if I were super glued to it. A police officer came around the counter and saw me sitting on the floor frozen.

"Get off the floor," as he smirked. "We waited at the front to see if the man you described returned, and he did."

I felt a chill run down my spine and was grateful the police caught him. "He did indeed have a rifle on him, but he has a permit, so we did not arrest him."

What!? What planet am I on?

"He threatened to kill me. Why would you let him go?"

The officer shifted his stance and was obviously irritated I would question his decision-making.

"I suggest you grab your stuff and leave the store. You don't belong here."

With pleasure jackass. I happily followed his direction and left the store immediately.

Months passed with no further visits from Len. I relinked with my friend Nicol, and we renewed our friendship. It felt so easy, like we never missed a beat. She told me Len recently called her, and they had a conversation. She said he was hired on with the Mason police department and just met a woman he had fallen in love with.

I began to cry and thanked God he found someone else and now he would leave me alone. That's exactly what happened, I never heard from Len again.

Chapter Ten

"You must find the place inside yourself where nothing is impossible."

~ ***Deepak Chopra***

The winters in Indiana were long and bitter cold. I longed to move back to the sunshine and warmer weather. I was not fond of the idea of leaving my father and living close to my mother, but I made my decision. I waited until I completed the current semester at college and made plans to move back to Florida. I told my mother of my plans, and she begged me to move in with her until I found my own place.

"Annie, it will give us a chance to get close and heal wounds. You will have your own room, and I will respect your space. Please come home."

I so wanted to believe her. I wanted a loving relationship with her. I agreed and began packing.

I again drove straight through to Florida with my car packed to the gills. I could not fit a toothpick in that car and had no idea how unsafe it was to drive 1500-miles not being able to see out the rear window. I settled in with my mother and immediately got a job at an athletic club serving food poolside and in their fine dining area. I made friends fast, and we partied every night after work. I enrolled at the local community college and was close to completing my associate degree.

I ran into a friend I went to high school with, and he was about to sit for the bar exam. We went to Junior prom together as friends, but he wanted a sexual relationship; I did not. He was the drum major in the marching band and was well respected by his peers and teachers. His dream was to be an attorney be eventually a judge, and he was well on his way. Rick was an intense guy, was always in control and domineering. His icy blue eyes could see right through you. We went out twice, but I soon realized it wasn't a relationship I wanted to continue. After ending things, he didn't handle the rejection well and I made it clear that I had no interest in seeing him again.

Little did I know when I left that evening to meet old friends from high school at the smoky pool hall that I was going to meet my future husband. Mitch was a friend two years ahead of me in high school. We were in the marching band together and he was active in the photography club. His brother, Max was two years older than him and had just graduated high school before I entered my freshman year. He was socially awkward, and clothes were wrinkled and mismatched, but he seemed very interested in me. It was not instant attraction, but it was a desire to get to know Max better. He was best friends with Rick, so I knew this would be a bit awkward. I confided in Max about going on a few dates with Rick, but I wasn't really into him. Max reassured me that it wouldn't affect their friendship at all.

We met for lunch the next day and became inseparable from that day onwards. When Rick found out, he left a voicemail in my machine stating he would get me back someday for rejecting him and then dating his best friend. It impacted the relationship between Rick and Max, but they mended fences two months later. Max was in a local community college with the goal of entering Florida State University (FSU) in his junior year. I knew if I were to continue dating Max and eventually marry, I would need to align my college courses and goals with his. We married one year after our first date and moved immediately to Tallahassee. Max entered FSU two months later, and I entered

Tallahassee Community College for the last semester of my AA program before entering the social work program at FSU.

Life with Max was easy and comfortable. We loved each other very much and discussed starting a family. One year into our marriage, I became pregnant. I was incredibly excited and nervous. I did a home pregnancy test while Max was in class at FSU. I could not wait to share the news with him. I jumped in my car and ran all over campus to find him in class. Two hours later, I found him and crashed into his classroom to pull him out. He was in shock and disbelief with the news. This quickly turned to joy for both of us and planning went into full gear. We mapped out our finances and continued our education. Six weeks into the pregnancy, I started spotting blood and had sporadic cramping. Worry set in and the doctor scheduled an appointment with us for the next day. The night dragged on for eternity as the cramping continued and intensified. We arrived at the doctor's office, and at this point I was in intense pain.

I needed to use the restroom in the waiting area, and this is where my pregnancy ended with a miscarriage. I was utterly devastated and felt gutted. I exited the restroom and fell into Max's arms sobbing.

The doctor insisted on an exam, but all I wanted was to go home and crawl up into a ball. The doctor patted me on the shoulder and said, "No worries. Try again in three months".

The following days slowly ticked by as I went through the motions of school and work. It was all my fault. God was punishing me for having an abortion at 16 years old. I have ruined my chances to have a family and all the years of arduous work in therapy will never pay off. My dream of having children and raising them with unconditional love would never be. I hated God, I hated my mother, I hated myself. I re-entered counseling to deal with my grief and anger.

Months later, I ended back at the campus doctor's office with abdominal pain. The doctor did a thorough examination, asked me to get dressed and we would 'talk'. I had no idea what would be discussed, and fear flooded my body. He said you have a sexually transmitted disease STD and need to talk to your husband.

It took what seemed like forever to process what was said and the only words I could utter was, "could I get an STD without one of us being with another person?"

The doctor responded with, "one of you has had sexual contact with another person infected with this specific STD."

The room started spinning and I became ill.

I arrived home and waited for Max to return from school. So many questions. Who was he seeing? Did I know her? Did he love her? In the days to follow, Max denied any sexual contact despite my relentless probing. I eventually conceded and decided to put this in a box and tuck it deep down inside of myself. I loved Max and needed him. Soon thereafter, I was pregnant with my son, Alexander. I held my breath for the first three months until I felt confident the pregnancy was viable. The first months were incredibly taxing on my health. I lost twenty pounds due to excessive nausea and vomiting. At one point, I vomited so hard I burst all the blood vessels around both eyes and my throat bled from being raw. I was down to 108 pounds at 5 '7 and the physician became concerned. I told him when I was hungry, I only ate fruits, vegetables, and protein to ensure I was eating as healthy as possible for the baby.

He said, "I want you eating peanut butter, ice cream, high fat and start putting on weight. If not, I'm placing you in the hospital."

A few weeks later the nausea ceased, and I made up for lost time. I had a banana split every day from the local Dairy Queen, and peanut butter banana sandwiches as often as possible. Max grew more distant and angrier. His obsession for watching sports on TV increased to the point of addiction. He lined up every TV in the house side by side and watched numerous games at the same time. If I questioned this behavior, his agitation with me grew. I would pray his favorite teams would win, as he would throw and brake things in the house if his team lost or fell behind. The screaming became constant every weekend and numerous weeknights. I found myself retreating to the bedroom to escape from temper tantrums in front of the televisions. The screaming would often trigger my PTSD and I began to fear Max.

The birth of Alexander was the most wonderful and challenging day of my life up to this point. My labor was long, 33 hours to be exact, and painful. My epidural did not numb my left side, only the right. At 30 hours my body was so exhausted, I was not responding as I should. My blood pressure became erratic, and my breathing was shallow. The doctor decided to use suction to remove the baby, but this failed. Next was forceps and this was only to be tried for a few minutes before transitioning to a C-Section. On the last push, Alexander arrived.

He was laid across my chest and I wept tears of absolute joy and exhaustion. God blessed me with a healthy son. The next 4 weeks was an extremely difficult healing process due to excessive tearing during labor. I could not stand upright without extreme pain. When Max was in school, I crawled throughout the house to get to where I needed to be. Staying horizontal to the floor was the only position I could tolerate.

I counted the hours until Max arrived home in hope to get help with the care of Alexander and household chores. Max expected to be cooked for and I was too concerned with pleasing him that I did not ask for help. Asking for help preceded anger, rejection, and shame. It was a perpetual fear of him leaving me that asking for my own needs was not acceptable; a self-imposed rule ingrained from childhood. If he loved me, he would see how much I was suffering and would take care of me and his son. I expected him to read my mind or come to this realization on his own.

Four weeks later, I went for my post-birth checkup and removal of stitches. The doctor looked utterly shocked as he examined me. He saw my worry and gently said, "your stitches fell out unexpectedly and you have not healed at all."

He then said he would have to cauterize the wound closed as stitches were no longer an option. The procedure was archaic and humiliating. No pain medication was given and the smell of burning flesh was nauseating. I felt traumatized and violated as I clothed and left his office.

Alexander's first 3 months of life were difficult for him. He suffered from colic and jaundice. He cried for the majority of the day and could not get comfortable. Once I healed, I would swaddle him against my chest and jog throughout the apartment. Around the dining room table, through the living room and into the kitchen. This is the only thing that seemed to comfort him. When he was happy, I would dress him in his sweet outfits and take hundreds of pictures. His sweet smile and loving gaze were the joy of my life. As we sat in the rocking chair, I sang to him until he fell asleep, swaying back and forth with the gentle motion of the chair.

When Alexander was 8 weeks old, I started my master's Advanced Standing program at FSU. It was an accelerated intensive program for students that graduated with honors with their bachelor's degree. Currently, I was struggling with postpartum depression. My physical pain was subsiding, as the emotional pain crept in.

Max graduated and got a job as a computer programmer. His job sent him out of state for one week for training. We stayed in touch every night by phone and the day before his scheduled return he announced he was staying two extra days to attend a couple sporting events. Holding the phone against my ear while rocking Alexander in the rocking chair, I begged him not to stay as I was so exhausted, minimal sleep and could not stop crying; he refused and called me selfish. We ended the call, and I gazed down at my beautiful boy swaddled in his favorite blanket and wondered how I could keep going. His eyes gave me strength. I would need to dig deep and move forward.

The months ticked by, and tension increased. Alexander would be in his bouncy seat happily playing with toys and watching Max animated in front of the television. The explosions were often and without warning. The referee would make a bad call and Max would melt down. Alexander would start screaming in fear and I would run in and scoop him up. I told Max he needed to get his anger under control, and he snapped. He spun around, ripped the eyeglasses off his face, smashed them to pieces in his hand, threw them on the floor and got inches from my face screaming at the top of his lungs, "Don't tell me what to do, Alexander can deal with it, and you can too! All he does is scream anyways."

Often, there was remorse at the end of the day, with requests for me to be more patient and understanding.

We decided to move back home at the end of my master's program to be closer to family and their support. In May, I was accepted by a community mental health agency in Naples to complete my master's internship. Max secured a job in Naples, so we packed up and moved home to our new apartment rental. We pulled into the driveway of our new home and were welcomed by Max's mother and father-in-law. As we unloaded the truck, Max's mother, Jan asked me if I was pregnant. I was shocked by the question and inquired as to why she asked. She responded, "you just seem tired, that's all." I could not sleep that night thinking about her question. The next morning, I ran to the pharmacy and brought home a pregnancy test. I impatiently wanted the 15 minutes for the results- pregnant.

Joy and fear gripped me. Joy of another beautiful child to call my own. Fear of another difficult pregnancy and if Max could adapt to another child. I shared the information with Max that evening and he looked perplexed. I asked what he was thinking. He looked me square in eye and said, "I don't think I can love another child the way I love Alexander."

Little did I know at that moment, this would be the theme for years to come.

***

The pregnancy was easy and joyous; feeling life growing inside me was a miraculous gift from God. I was hired after my internship with the community mental health agency; the same unit I was on for three days as a 16-year-old. I worked in the crisis unit doing rounds with a psychiatrist seeing patients under a 72-hour psychiatric hold. The job was educational and stressful. I was constantly vigilant of my proximity to actively psychotic patients while I was pregnant. Many fellow employees were attacked and injured while on the unit. I often narrowly escaped an attack and frequently questioned my option to stay on the job or request a change in position. I would share my fears with Max, and he offered little more than a shrug of the shoulders.

At eight months pregnant, I was walking through the unit and back to the nurse's station. One of the patients, who was actively experiencing psychosis and often visited the unit, managed to evade my attention and suddenly appeared in front of me. It took me by surprise as I had not realized he was approaching. He dropped to his knees in front of me and placed both hands on either side of my very pregnant belly. He gazed up and looked into my eyes and raised his finger up to his lips.

"Shhhhh, baby Jesus is talking to me", he whispered. He laid his head on the top of my belly as I stood paralyzed in fear.

My eyes darted around the unit and into the nurse's station. Where are the unit techs? Where are the nurses? Why aren't they out here helping me? The patient continued to speak to my belly and chanted biblical verses in Haitian which I could not understand. The nurse finally saw what was happening on the unit and called for backup.

Within seconds, the patient was pulled off me and taken to isolation and medicated. I was left shaken and afraid to go back on to the unit. The fear was not really for me, but for my baby and my inability to protect him if attacked. Money was extremely tight at this point, and I needed to continue working up until I went into labor. Taking time off work was not a luxury we could afford at this point. My due date came and went. My anticipation to have my baby grew.

Andrew was born two weeks past his due date, and I worked until the day before I went to the hospital to induce labor. The delivery was much different with Andrew. With being induced, contractions came on fast and furious. Max left the room often to watch a football game on a TV in the lobby. I felt furious, betrayed, and abandoned by this and told the nurse to bring him in before he misses the birth of his son.

Within three hours, Andrew came into this world. I waited for him to be placed on my chest like Alexander was, but it was not happening. The doctor and nurses whispered as they worked feverishly at my feet. I did not hear the beautiful first cry of my beautiful son.

A wave of panic washed over me, and I screamed out "What's wrong? Why isn't he crying?"

The doctor responded, "The umbilical cord was wrapped around his neck. We are stimulating him."

I sat up on the table and saw his lifeless body, purple and limp. The nurse pushed me back down on the table and assured me all was fine.

He was moved to another part of the room and onto a table. The doctor continued to stimulate him until he got a response. What seemed like hours, I finally heard his first cry. Tears of joy and relief flowed down my cheeks. It took hours before I was allowed to hold Andrew in my arms as he was being closely monitored and treated. Once in my arms, my heart was full. His beautiful round cheeks, tiny fingers, and toes. He was a miracle.

We brought Andrew home and introduced him to Alexander. I placed him gently in his brother's waiting arms and the bond was immediate. I sat in wonder as I tried to comprehend how incredibly blessed I was to have two healthy, beautiful sons.

Max and I set our sights on buying a home. Now we were both working on our careers, have a growing family, and desired a home of our own. I found a great home in a family-oriented community immediately. We made an offer and moved in within weeks.

Tension grew between Max and me. I often told him I needed more help from him with the kids and the household. My requests were often rejected, stating "I make more money than you. You need to pick up the slack in household and kid duties."

He would get home from work later and later and expected dinner to be waiting for him. Once I picked up both kids from daycare after work, I went home, fed them, bathed them, cooked dinner, and waited for Max to arrive home. Dinner was left in the oven to stay warm, but Max refused to eat it.

"I consider that leftovers, and I don't eat leftovers!"

My shock turned to anger, and I said, "I will continue to make us dinner, if you choose not to eat it, that is your choice, and you can make your own."

Max again, called me selfish and stated he would be happy to make his own dinner. Out of defiance, he made himself Eggo waffles every night for months. The distance and resentments between us grew like a cancer.

Andrew was such a happy and joyful baby. He slept through the night quickly and always had a sweet smile on his face. He laughed and giggled watching Alexander dance around him in circles trying to make him laugh. I often would catch myself staring at the two of them together and wondered how on earth I was so blessed to get two wonderful, loving children. They were truly a gift from God. A gift I would always cherish.

Alexander went in for a regular check up with the pediatrician. The doctor expressed concern over the discrepancy between Alexander's head growth and his body growth. She stated he needs to have an MRI to rule out a brain tumor. Absolute fear gripped me, and the room started to spin. A brain tumor?

That night, I sat down with Max to discuss her findings and review costs.

Max said, "That is ridiculous. He just has a big head like I do. We are not spending $1,000 on an MRI to tell us nothing is wrong!"

What? I wanted to reach across the table and scratch his eyes out.

"Let me make this crystal clear, he will have an MRI and if I have to take him without you knowing, that's exactly what I will do!"

He was insistent this was not going to happen. The next day, I scheduled the appointment for the following day. Max was absolutely beside himself furious with me.

To have a toddler sit still long enough to get an accurate MRI is quite a feat. It was scheduled for his bedtime in hopes he would be tired enough to fall asleep before being placed on the table. Max begrudgingly came to the appointment and stood in the corner with his arms folded in front of him and a scowl on his face. It took a couple days before the results came in. The pediatrician called and reported there was no evidence of a tumor. Alexander was fine. I sobbed on the phone and hung up to share the news with Max.

He glared at me and said, "I told you so. What a waste of money! So dumb." I knew at that moment; our marriage was ending.

The distance grew between us. My life was work, children, housework. His life was work and televised sports. I continued to ask him to be an active participant in the marriage and help with the needs of us and our home. He always answers that he does enough and for me to get over it. My anger and resentment grew, and his disinterest became more apparent.

I told Max I was no longer happy in the marriage and that I needed more from him. I asked if he would grocery shop once a month to help take some of the household burden off me; he refused. At this point, we were almost roommates. I wanted just one effort to be made on his part to tell me he was invested in saving our marriage.

I relied increasingly on my friendships for emotional support and social fulfillment. These were relationships made at work because this was the only time I had to communicate with others. Sarah, the receptionist at the mental health unit where I worked, was my best friend. She had a daughter the same as Alexander's age, and her marriage was on shaky ground as well.

Bob and I worked closely for 3 years, and we became great friends. His relationship with his wife was ending as well and we spent hours talking about our issues and frustrations. Our relationship slowly shifted from friendship to more of an emotional relationship. We often said we could not have a romantic relationship unless we both were no longer married. It was challenging to keep boundaries with Bob as I was so unhappy with Max for years of disrespect and neglect. Bob and I started talking and seeing each other outside of work. I knew how wrong this was, but I was desperate for care and understanding.

I eventually told Max we needed to try couples counseling, or we had to separate. He reluctantly agreed and we attended numerous sessions with a couple's therapist. I begged Max to check back into the marriage and move away from the hours spent watching sporting events. The therapist asked Max to fulfill my request of grocery shopping once a month and we would build from there; Max refused. The therapist stated this would show your wife you care and are invested in the marriage. He again said his income compensated me for my extra work.

After numerous sessions Max reluctantly agreed to this. He went once with a detailed list written by me and he came home with half the items written on the list. I was instructed ahead of time by the therapist to show praise if this were to happen; I did. Next session, Max refused to do this again.

The therapist finally looked at us and said, "you need to get a divorce.

Max is stuck in his family of origin and needs a mother. You have moved on from your family of origin and created a family. You need a partner, not another child to care for."

I was speechless, and Max became angry. We left the therapists' office and did not speak for days.

The end came when he became angry with the loss of his favorite college team. I told him I cannot take it anymore with the screaming. Max ran up to me as I backed up against the bedroom door. He got right up to my face and said he was done, then smashed a hole through the bedroom door, inches from my face. I crawled into bed and planned my exit plan. I called my attorney the next day and told her what happened. She advised me and the boys to leave immediately for my safety. My plan was to wait until the next weekend when Max went to work, I would pack any clothes, some of the kids' clothes and their needs, and flee to my mother's home. I would file for divorce, stay with my mother for a couple of months with the kids until I could save enough money to get an apartment. I left a note for Max telling him I left with the kids, that we would be at my mother's, and we could discuss a schedule for him to see the kids.

I waited all night for a phone call or for Max to show up at my mother's home in a rage. I was prepared and had all doors locked. He did not call or come over. I was totally shocked by this. What would be the next step? Max called the next day and asked to see the kids that evening; I reluctantly agreed. They spent the night, and I retrieved them the next day. Still, no discussion about the separation.

My attorney filed for divorce, temporary custody, and temporary child support, and to set up a parenting schedule. Max hired his best friend as his attorney, and he vowed to have me eviscerated in court. My attorney assured me this was a no brainer based on the lack of involvement with the kids and marriage, and Max's anger issues.

Max and I set up a temporary schedule per our attorney's request until a hearing took place. Both attorneys suggested a 50/50 shared schedule with every two-day rotation. I did not want to agree to this, by my attorney assured this was only temporary and the court will amend at the hearing.

The court date quickly arrived and what was supposed to be a 20-minute court session with our attorneys speaking for us, turned into a murder trial for me. Max's attorney hired an independent court reported which was not standard procedure and ordered that I testify on the stand.

My mother was present. The kids were at daycare, and it was my turn to pick them up after court. His mother and brother were present and the glares from them was unnerving. His attorney was overconfident, and my attorney reminded me this would be quick and painless 20-minute hearing.

She said "Look, the courtroom is packed with cases for the judge to hear. When he calls your name, we will present the issue, he will render his order, and we are done. You will have temporary custody and child support ordered."

I nodded and waited nervously in my seat.

I was the first to take the stand. His attorney, Max's best friend, Rick approached the bench and looked me deep in the eyes and smiled, almost salivating for what was to unfold. I remember the voicemail he had left on my machine seven years prior stating he would get me back someday. Today was the day. My attorney started with the questioning.

She asked basic questions at first and then asked how we currently shared time with the kids. She then asked how this was going. I responded I saw changes in Alexander, as well as his teacher and I request for the kids to be with me full time for consistency. She rested, and Max's attorney approached the bench. He asked a few basic questions, but it soon turned into an inquiry about my mental state. My attorney objected but court allowed the questioning. I responded that I had been diagnosed with depression. He then asked if I was ever committed as a patient for mental health treatment.

I responded "yes, when I was 16 years old."

I was then asked if I took medication for this mental illness, and I responded I took Prozac for depression. He then asked if I was ever a victim of child abuse. I was shocked. How was this relevant to a temporary custody hearing?

I looked at my attorney, waiting for an objection, but it never came. I looked at my mother as her eyes dropped to her lap.

I responded, "Yes."

I was asked by whom, I responded, "My mother."

"Is this the same mother you and the kids are currently residing with?" he asked.

I responded "Yes."

"No further questions," he nodded to the judge, and then glared at me.

It was Max's turn on the stand. His attorney asked basic questions. He was asked if he had ever been treated for a mental health issue. Max responded "no." He was asked if anyone from his family or friends who watches the kids had ever abused kids. Max responded "no." Max then stated he just wants to see his kids 50 percent of the time.

My attorney then cross-examined. She asked, "Do you have a problem with your wife having the kids?"

Max responded "No."

She asked, "Are you alleging that the grandmother has ever abused your two children?"

Max responded "No."

This was the end of her questioning. That was it? That was all she had to ask him? Well, at least Max spoke the truth which negated his attorneys arduous work of painting a horrific picture of me and my 'mental illness.'

A parenting coordinator was then discussed to review a plan for visitation. Max's attorney then sited numerous cases regarding stability since I moved out of the home to my mother's home, then plan to move to my own home once finances permit in a few months. It was argued Max lives in the marital home, thus can provide more stability. He then cited court cases that if a parent suffered from child abuse, it was likely that the adult would abuse their children.

My attorney refuted his case findings and deemed them irrelevant. The judge decided we would share custody and since Max had the ability to pay $1,200 monthly child support based on his income, he was to do so. I was also awarded primary custodial parent. Max just seethed contempt for me, and his attorney was deflated. They filed an appeal on the order for child support before leaving the courtroom.

I walked out of the courtroom feeling humiliated and defeated. I had never dreamed the judge would order 50/50 temporary custody. My attorney swore it was a slam dunk that I would have full temporary custody due to his lack of involvement with the kids. I did not care about the child support. I just wanted my children full time. I had never in my days been as angry at Max as I was that day. To take my personal history that I shared with him during our marriage and have it spilled out in a packed, open courtroom was unconscionable. I no longer feared Max, I loathed him.

My mother and I had an awkward drive home. We never spoke about the issues revealed in court. She appeared remorseful but remained silent. I later picked up the boys from daycare and hugged them tighter than I ever had previously.

Max showed up that night at my mother's home in a rage. He pounded on the doors, front and back, demanding to be let in. I told him I would not answer the door unless he calmed down. This enraged him more. I told Max I was calling the police because he was trying to break through the glass door. Max screamed he would not pay me child support and that judge was a senile old man and should not be serving the court. He bellowed that he appealed the decision and will make me pay dearly. Max eventually left and the next few weeks were emotionally draining and filled with fear.

The boys were constantly dirty when I got them back on my days. I decided I would go back into the home if Max had not already changed the locks and see what the state of the house was. I was shocked at the filth. Food everywhere, dirty clothes all over the floor. Half-eaten raw hotdogs on plates in their bedrooms. I took pictures of everything in hopes this would help my case. I retrieved all the 'Precious Moments' figurines Max gave me for every birthday and holiday. I hated those things but never had the heart to tell him that. I took them to the pawn shop to try and get some money from them to pay my attorney fees, but the employee just laughed at me and said they were worthless.

That evening, I set up all the figurines in my mother's driveway, grabbed a baseball bat and asked my mother if she was willing to play baseball with me. Of course, she obliged. We spent the evening, her pitching figurines to me and me smashing them out of the park with my bat. It felt so good, small victories.

It was a beautiful sunny day, so the boys and I decided to wash my car. They had fun spraying each other and me with the hose. We piled inside and wiped down the dashboard, and Alexander collected his numerous Hot wheel cars off the backseat. Andrew opened my glovebox and found a small bag of peanuts. He shoved a handful in his mouth at the same time Alexander climbed into the front seat and honked the car horn. It startled Andrew so badly, he gasped and inhaled the mouthful of peanuts. I instantly grabbed him and ran inside, screaming to my mother what had happened. Andrew was barely breathing and grasping at his throat. My mother called 911 and the operator instructed we lay him down on the couch and keep him calm until the paramedics arrived.

After what felt like an eternity, but was only a few minutes, the paramedics finally arrived and began attending to Andrew.

I was pacing the floor, then hovering over the paramedics, shouting questions, "Is he breathing? Will he live? What is going on? Answer me, damn it!"

They were able to stabilize his breathing and we were transported to the hospital. A physician quickly evaluated him, and he stated they were not equipped to manage this kind of case, and Andrew would need to be transported to a children's hospital the next town over. We rode by ambulance to the neighboring town and a physician was waiting at the hospital entrance for us. He quickly evaluated Andrew and came back out to the lobby with two nurses and stated they needed to take him into surgery immediately.

I began trembling all over, as he turned away to prep Andrew for surgery. He turned back and saw the terror in my eyes. He walked back to me and took my hands in his.

"I will take good care of him. I have children of my own. I understand."

My eyes filled with tears, "Please Doctor. Please save my son."

With that, he was gone.

I looked around the waiting room and it was completely empty. The lights were dim, and it was now dark outside as it was the wee hours of the morning. My knees felt weak, and it took all I had not to fall to pieces. I walked over to a row of plastic chairs linked together and dropped to my knees. With my elbows on the seat of the chair and my hands clasped together in front of my face, I prayed like I have never prayed before in my life.

"Please God. I will do anything. Please do not let my son die. Please guide the surgeons' hands. I will sell my soul to the Devil himself if you just spare him."

A warm glow came over me as if God was sitting next to me. A sense of calm came over me and I knew He heard my prayers.

Why isn't Max here? I called him hours ago and told him what happened and where we were. I called him again but no answer. The hours slowly ticked by and I wore a path in the hard floor of the hospital waiting room.

The surgeon finally came out and I ran up to meet him. He smiled and said, "You've got a strong boy there. He did wonderfully and he is in recovery."

I burst out sobbing and tried to control my emotions. He went on to say, "This was a tricky surgery as peanuts are the worst type of food that can be inhaled. Peanuts dissolve with body heat, then saturate the lining of the lungs slowly cutting off the air supply. So, we had to go in and scrape the melted peanut butter out of the lungs without damaging the lining."

I expressed my eternal gratitude for his care and skill. Within two hours, Andrew was up and out of the hospital bed running down the hallways. The doctors and nurses were absolutely amazed. I lifted my eyes up and whispered, "Thank you."

The days without the children were almost unbearable. I could not focus on work. I came home and sat staring at their empty beds. The pain was almost debilitating. I found myself turning to wine on the days the boys were with Max in efforts to numb the pain. If I drank enough, the pain subsided but left me with remorse the next day.

My relationship with Bob jumped from friendship to romance. He was going through the same despair and heartbreak. I felt desperate for the love and comfort of a man. Someone to take the pain away. Someone to hold me up as I was spiraling into a deep depression.

Eight weeks later, my mother said it was time to go. She could not take the noise and disruption any longer. Max hadn't made any child support payments until that point despite the court order. His assumption that submission of an appeal afforded him the right to not pay and would die before he gave me a penny. I informed him he was in contempt, so he had to pay until his appeal was reviewed.

We had agreed to leave our joint bank account in place, and it was only to be used for groceries until the judge instructed us at the final hearing on how to split it up. Max decided to empty our account after the temporary hearing to pay for his attorney. I found out about this while checking out at the grocery store and my bank card was declined. I did not have any other form of payment, so had to leave the store without food.

I obtained a credit card and found a tiny, two-bedroom guest house on the north end of town. No washer and dryer, but it was clean and safe. I negotiated a deal with the landlord to decrease the security deposit and allow us to move in quickly. We moved in and made it a home. The boys were happy and told me about getting a pet bunny. Max drove by numerous times a day checking to see if I had company. Max was convinced I was having a steamy affair with Bob and was bound to catch him at my home. Sometimes, I would sit on the front porch and wave as Max drove by. Max's attorney threatened to subpoena Bob to attend our final hearing in efforts to prove an inappropriate relationship to tarnish my character and decrease any alimony payment that may be ordered. Max found it easy and comfortable to blame this relationship as to the reason the marriage dissolved. The inability to take accountability for his behavior was astonishing but not surprising.

I continued to drink wine on the days when the boys were away. Many times, I fell asleep on the kitchen floor with my bible as a pillow. I begged God for the pain to end. For my children to come back full time. For someone to love me.

The final hearing date was set and quickly approaching. I was absolutely dreading it since I was still traumatized by the first hearing.

My attorney continued to assure me I would obtain full custody and Max will have weekly visitation.

Max called me at work and said he was done fighting me. He would give me full custody if I agreed he did not need to pay child support. I fervently nodded my head in agreement, then hung up the phone and collapsed onto the floor, sobbing uncontrollably. My boss sent me home because I could not stop crying.

The fight was over. My boys were going to be with me full time. The next few days were total bliss.

***

On a Saturday, I picked up the boys at the home because Alexander was sick and wanted to be with me. Max looked at me and fell to his knees. He was crying and stated he realized his mistakes and how irresponsible he was. He begged me to come back and work things out. I looked at him sobbing on the floor and felt nothing but contempt. After all those years that I begged for help, after all the times he chose sports over family, after what he did to me in court and paint me as a mentally unstable person. The ship had sailed. It was too little too late. I asked him to enter counseling to be a better parent.

Everything was looking up until the next phone call. Max stated he spoke with his sister-in-law, and she urged him to fight for full custody and hope for 50/50. Max shared she felt sons needed a father more than every other weekend. He said he will fight me to the bitter end and that he would not stop until I was paying him child support. I told him this was due to me rejecting his apology and now he wanted to punish me. He laughed and said I will regret that decision.

Max's attorney filed a motion to resolve outstanding issues before the final hearing. It was proposed 50|50 custody, he would pay half child support, keep the home and buy me out, and we would split home furnishings. The proposal further stated if I did not agree, Bob would be ordered to court to state what his relationship was with me. I notified my attorney I would not accept any deal that does not include full custody for me. We sent notice that we rejected the proposal.

Mediation was then scheduled to see if we could come to an agreement before the final hearing. At mediation, it again was proposed 50/50 custody and half child support. It was agreed upon that Max would keep the house since I could not afford it on my own and he would pay off the rest of my student loans. I would keep my car, we would split furnishings, and we would split our debt. The last issue was custody. I would not budge on 50/50 custody. I was willing to concede to child support if I was given full custody; he refused.

The final hearing was still scheduled, and his attorney then filed for full custody and child support payments. I was ready. I planned to fight until my last breath. We completed a court mandated child evaluation and parenting class. The judge now had all the requested information she needed, and a 10-minute hearing was on the docket for next week. It was the longest week of my life. I was hopeful yet terrified.

The hearing was brief and full of contention. The judge chastised us for not coming to an agreement in mediation and to take up the courts time with this nonsense. She rendered her order- shared 50/50 custody and Max to pay half child support. The judge stated based on the evaluations and our history that we were both good parents and able to care for our children.

I burst out of my seat and yelled at the judge, "You can't do that. He does not know how to care for them! He feeds them raw hotdogs and crackers. They are allowed to stay up until all hours of the night. He is unable to set boundaries. The house is disgusting and dirty; I have pictures to prove it. He has never cut their fingernails, scheduled a doctor appointment. Heck, he doesn't even know the name of their doctor."

The judge was incensed by my outburst. She banged her gavel and barked back at me, "Well he will have to learn now won't he!"

My attorney grabbed my arm and pulled me back into my chair. The judge then reprimanded Max for not paying any child support that was previously ordered by the court and will garnish his wages due to this. My mind went blank, the walls closed in, my attorney was speaking, but I could not hear her words.

I walked out of the courtroom May 1, 2001, picked up the kids from daycare then drove home. My life would never be the same. My children were stolen from me. My heart was broken. Traumatized and dissociated and, I went for a walk while my mother watched the boys. I walked down the street like a zombie, hearing the judge's words echoing in my mind. I just did not understand. I could not comprehend. I just lost the most important human beings to me. I crawled into a neighbor's ditch and waited for the earth to swallow me whole period in a fetal position I looked up at the sky and waited for God to tell me why, why would this happen to me?

The only thing I heard was silence. The ground was warm and wet under me, and a hawk circled a buzz above me as if sizing up a possible meal. As quick as the judge's gavel hit the bench, I snatched back to reality and became aware of my surroundings. I must get out of this ditch. God, what if the neighbors are looking out the window? Cars are whizzing by, but no one stopped. Did they see me? I got to my knees and climbed out of the ditch and navigated home. I stumbled home, feeling disheveled and out of sorts. My entire world was gathered at the dining table, lost in the task of coloring a picture for their mother. I decided I would do everything I could to protect them from their father's poor parenting and lack of boundaries. And what a journey it would be.

During this time, I saw less and less of Bob until he confided he was going to move out of his friend's home, and back in with his wife to repair his marriage. I was happy for both of them although it was bittersweet. I knew our friendship had come to an end. For his marriage to work, all communications must cease. It would be years before I ever laid eyes on him again.

Chapter Eleven

"Nothing ever goes away until it teaches us what we need to know."
~ ***Pema Chodron***

In July, I took the kids to my friend, Sarah's home to play with her daughter. There, I saw her brother, Ted working on his car in the garage. Sarah spoke about him in the past, but this will be the first time we meet. He showed the boys what he was working on, and they had fun learning various parts of a car.

Ted asked me out on a date, and I reluctantly agreed. I was still so raw from the divorce but wanting to see where this could go. Sarah begged me not to date him and stated he could be a real jerk. I told her I would make that decision for myself.

Ted and I went on numerous dates, he enjoyed spending time with the boys. They built model cars and went fishing. Ted provided all the things the young boys needed that Max did not. I did see a few reds flags with Ted but chose not to pay attention to them as he seemed to genuinely care about me and the boys.

In September, I discovered I was pregnant with William. I was terrified and did not want to go through the pregnancy without a solid commitment. Ted and I got engaged and found a large home to rent together. Things were all falling into place. A supportive man who loved me and my children, and another child on the way. The night we moved in Ted was putting things away in the garage. The boys were fast asleep in their new beds. I came out and asked him to finish up so we could spend time together. He spun on his heels and threw the wrench he was holding. He looked me square in the face, and said, "Fuck you. Do not tell me what to do. Get your ass in the house and I will be there when I get there."

I stood motionless and was at a loss for words.

I later met with Sarah and talked about what happened. She did not seem surprised. She stated when Ted was married before, he beat up his 13-year-old stepson for talking back. He was arrested and mandated to anger management classes. I was blown away. I asked her why she had never shared this with me, and she said it was not her business to say.

The next day was September 11, 2001. I stood in the middle of the psychiatric unit I worked on and watched the twin towers fall on television. I ran to pick up the boys from daycare as I did not know what was happening in the world. I felt an overwhelming need to get them and protect them.

I spent the rest of the evening in disbelief while we watched the media coverage of the terrorist attacks. I rubbed my belly and wondered if this world would even feel safe again. Ted's anger increased towards me, and his verbal abuse increased dramatically. I told Ted it was over and started packing to move. I had no idea where I would go, but I needed to leave before Ted became cruel to my children.

At this time, Max and I were talking more civilly and fell into a decent pattern of communication. Max stated if you move back in with me, we can work on things, and I will help you raise your baby. We would be roommates and attend counseling to see if we could ever have a relationship. I felt desperate to get away from Ted and had no money at the time. I met Max at the house, and we discussed the plan further. I shared with Ted that I was moving in with Max and we would see where our relationship goes. Ted was livid. I think he would have killed me at that point if I was not pregnant with his child.

The day I moved my belongings in, Max and I stood in the kitchen finalizing our plan and confirming our status as roommates.

Max looked at me and said, "But before you move in, you need to get an abortion. I decided I will not raise another man's child."

I stood there in total disbelief. How could I have ever trusted him again? I told him I would never even consider that as an option and that I made a huge mistake even entertaining the idea of possible reconciliation.

He smirked, and said, "Oh well, then you are out".

Two days later I found an apartment and with the help of friends, moved me and the kids in. Money was so incredibly tight. Max was not paying child support and I was too afraid to go back to court to enforce it. I could not go through another hearing again, and he knew it. Ted would periodically stop by and ask how I was doing with the pregnancy. He often asked to get back together but I told him that would never happen unless he got intensive counseling for his anger issues.

I had recently dropped off Alexander and Andrew at school and was headed into work for the day. I came to a stop in my minivan at a red light and glanced up in my rear-view mirror. I caught sight of the large work truck barreling towards the back of my van. The driver was looking down as if he dropped something on his floorboard. He smashed into the back of me going fifty-five miles per hour and hit me so hard my head flew forward then back against the headrest so hard; I broke the metal plate inside the headrest. I was shoved into the intersection and was gratefully not hit by another car.

An ambulance was called, and I was strapped onto a board and taken to the emergency room. I kept screaming to undo the strap across my forehead holding my head tightly to the backboard. The back of my head was swelling from the impact and the pressure was excruciating.

I grabbed my stomach and kept repeating, "I'm pregnant, I'm pregnant. Is my baby okay?"

Recovery from the accident was difficult. The force from the impact injured my back and I was diagnosed with three bulging vertebrates in my upper, middle, and lower back. Pregnant, alone, in pain, working a job that was burning me out, and in a financial crisis. How was I going to make it through this? I reluctantly called my mother to ask for help, but she was not interested in discussing my needs. She was blissfully happy planning a trip to Australia as her inheritance from her mother's estate has been recently settled. I hung up the phone and never felt more alone in my entire life.

Our downstairs neighbor was constantly pounding on my door, yelling to have my kids stop running around the apartment. He was sick and tired of the noise above him and would sue me if I did not control them better. Life was incredibly difficult for me. I barely made enough money to pay rent and the bills.

I came home one day to find an eviction notice taped to my front door due to the rent being three weeks late. Earlier that day, I stood in line at the local church to get food since I did not have enough money to eat. Max was still refusing to pay child support and I was drowning in credit card debt. He refused to pay for daycare, so most of my paycheck went to daycare so I could continue going to work. What a nasty cycle- work to pay for daycare. Daycare so I could go to work. Truly little left over. I picked up the phone and called a charity asking for help with rent. The same charity I stand in line with my destitute clients trying to get them services.

They came to my home, two workers and reviewed my situation. They offered to pay two months' rent, gave me a voucher for food and paid my past due electric bill. I was eternally grateful and full of shame I could not support my family despite working full time at a job I went through 6 years of college to get. How did I get here? Why did I continue to pick men that were angry and abusive? I knew I needed to continue working hard to heal the childhood wounds I had through counseling to stop the unhealthy pattern I was creating in my life. I reached out to a therapist and scheduled an appointment.

I ended up developing pneumonia from the stress of trying to keep everything together. I became so sick I could not get out of bed one morning and called my mother to help get the kids ready for school. She arrived, looked at me then called 911. My lips were blue, and I was short of breath. I was admitted to the maternity ward at the hospital to receive specialized care due to being pregnant. I spent 5 long days in the hospital recovering until I was well enough to be discharged home. It took two months to fully recover. I was terrified what this may be doing to the baby growing inside of me; gravely ill and all the antibiotic they pumped into me, being in a bad car accident, and constant stress.

My current relationship with my mother was a strained one. She fluctuated between supportive and shaming. I absolutely hated asking her for financial support, but on the occasion I did, she took the opportunity to call me pathetic and needy. She reminded me she does not want to be a bag lady who would be homeless someday, so she needed to watch her pennies. At the same time, she was a compulsive spender of material items with an extremely healthy bank account. Afterall, she soaked her last four husbands of their savings and was left a hefty sum after her mother's death.

"Mom, I'm certain you will not end up as a bag lady on the streets."

She responded, "Well, you never know. My four children do not care about me. You know Annie, all I ever wanted in life is children that loved me, and I will never have that. What an absolute disappointment," she sighed.

I wanted to scream, *"No amount of love would ever be enough for you. You're lucky three out of four of your children even want anything to do with you after the hell you put us through!"*

I could not utter the words. They stayed trapped in my throat and would be for years to come.

I was 8 months pregnant when I woke up in the middle of the night. The apartment building next to mine was on fire. A jealous man beat up his girlfriend, set the place on fire and left her to die. The flames came incredibly close to our unit. I thought to myself I must get out of here before I get sued by the man downstairs, or some lunatic sets my apartment complex on fire.

I saw an ad in the paper for a three-bedroom home almost across from the boys' school. I packed them up in the car and we went to look at it. It was owned by a lovely Christian couple that was moving out in a week. They saw me 8 months pregnant, no husband, with two kids ages 4 and 5, and desperate.

They lowered the rent, allowed me to pay first and last over a three-month period and handed me the keys. I went home, fell to my knees and thanked God for His mercy.

I did not have enough money for a mover, so I rented a truck and moved everything myself. I thought for sure I would go into labor early with all the heavy lifting, but I did not. We had a great backyard, a park that was only a street over and security.

Max called angrily and seethed, "If you move one more time in a short period of time, I am taking you back to court. The kids need stability and you're not providing it!"

Stability? He was lecturing me on stability and providing for my children?

"How dare you threaten me and preach about stability when you can't set limits, don't take them to a doctor, don't pack a lunch, send them to school with dirty clothes, failed to pay child support, ignore them by staying inside and watching sports all weekend, etc."

He knew the prospect of court terrified me and he held it over my head like a 100 lb. weight. He also knew he did not have to pay his mandated child support since I would never go back to court to enforce it.

Max bellowed, "I'm putting that support money in a prepaid school fund so the kids will have money for college. They will never have to worry about loans or debt."

As much as I needed the financial support now, I was pleased at least they would have money set aside for their future education.

I woke up two weeks later to my water having broken in the middle of the night. I got up, cooked breakfast for the boys, took them to school and packed my bags for the hospital. I called a friend to tell her my water broke last night, and she was frantic for me to get to the hospital. I called my job and told them I would not be coming in today. I debated if I should call Ted to let him know that I was in labor. I decided it was the right thing to do and he offered to drive me to the hospital.

I was admitted into the maternity wing and contractions were not strong enough yet to be in active labor. The doctor informed me that the baby needed to be delivered within 24 hours of water breaking, so we needed to induce labor. I remembered from my pregnancy with Andrew that contractions would come quickly from being induced, and this time was no different. My sweet William was born four hours later with no complications.

The nurse immediately laid William in my arms and all my stress and worries faded away. He was a perfectly pink and healthy baby boy. Ted stayed for the labor and had tears in his eyes as he gazed down on William. Ted begged me to allow William to be a part of his life and to work on repairing our relationship. I told him he could visit William, but a relationship was out of the question.

Two days later, William, Alexander, Andrew, and I arrived back home. I had six weeks of maternity leave and planned to use every second bonding with William and spending quality time with my three sons. In that period, I would also have to plan for William's care so I could return to work.

The daycare Alexander and Andrew went to had a long wait list, and I knew I could not afford it anyway. Ted's mother offered to babysit while I was at work. I was reluctant, for the reason that Ted and his mother had a very strained relationship, but that was all I could afford at the time. After a few months, I came to her home after work to pick up William and he was laying on a couch, soaked in urine, screaming. Ted's mother was in her room sleeping. I had no idea how long William was laying there without care or supervision. I grabbed him and ran out of the house. I told Ted he would never be in his mother's care again. I found another daycare across town that had openings and William started there right away.

William attended this daycare for a few months until I received a call from them one morning stating William would not stop crying and they did not know what was wrong. The caregiver said that she would continue to try and soothe William and would call back if I needed to pick him up. I did not hear back from them the rest of the day, so I assumed all was well.

I picked up William and he was exhausted. She said he has been out of it for a couple hours but seemed okay. He had dark circles under his eyes from crying and he was whimpering on the way home. I immediately took his shoes off and prepared a warm bath, and I then saw why William spent the day crying. When a caregiver put his shoe back on after playing, she jammed it on so hard, his pinky toe folded backwards and was laying across the side of his foot. Incredibly, they did not think to remove the shoe and examine his foot.

I arrived at the daycare the next morning without William and resisted grabbing that caregiver by the throat. I chewed her out one side and down the other, then filed a complaint with Department of Children and Families. Now, where do I find another daycare that can take William by tomorrow? The pit in my stomach grew, as the bills were piling up again and I needed to work.

William was not hitting milestones at the same rate as Alexander and Andrew. He choked on baby food when I tried to transition him from bottle to jarred food. He rocked back and forth, and he would bang his head against the back of his car seat. His pediatrician was unsure as to what was happening to William and told me to be patient with his lack of progress.

William started with a cold and was just not getting relief from his symptoms. His pediatrician recommended over the counter cold medicine and to keep him home for a couple of days. William progressively got worse, and it ended up with a trip to the emergency room for treatment. William was diagnosed with Respiratory Syncytial Virus RSV and was admitted to the children's unit at the hospital. I informed Ted and he arrived as a support. William was so sick, and I was terrified. He spent the next 5 days receiving breathing treatments and strong antibiotics. On day six, he was discharged to home. I was exhausted and emotionally drained.

Postpartum depression seeped in again and I was having difficulty even functioning. I again, picked up wine to help medicate the pain. I was taking an anti-depressant and seeing a therapist to help pull myself out of this hole. The depression intensified to a point that I sat down and wrote goodbye letters to each family member and my three sons. I then found myself in the sporting section of a department store asking if they sold guns so I could buy one. I was frequently in a state of dissociation and became paranoid my children would be taken away from me. I critically needed intervention but was too afraid Max would use this as an excuse to take me back to court. I was already painted as a mental case; this would seal it for me.

My sister, Louise whom I was not remarkably close with called me and asked me to come over; I refused. She would not take no for an answer and to bring a bathing suit, so angrily I went. We got in her pool, and I sat and cried for 7 hours straight. She gave me privacy but monitored me through her kitchen window. I do not think she realized she saved my life that day.

I continued to try off and on with Ted to make things work between us. He would arrive at my home and make promises that he saw the light and had changed his ways, I would occasionally fall for it. He would be kind for a few weeks, then revert to anger and demeaning behavior.

He continuously asked if he could move in, and the answer was consistently and emphatically "No."

I took every effort to keep him away from Alexander and Andrew. His time was limited with William. He was an expert at slowly and systematically wearing away a person's self-esteem and confidence. I could feel my body viscerally responding to this abuse and would then cut off communication for a period to recover. I eventually came to understand he was a narcissist and with this personality disorder, recovery would be long and intensive with consistent adherence to mental health counseling.

I eventually left the mental health crisis unit and was working at a place that treated the chronic mentally ill deinstitutionalized from the nearby state hospital. My job was to help keep them stable in the community, find housing, find them employment, fill medication boxes in their apartments and ensure they were medication compliant. It was a new community service agency, and they were trying to find their footing.

This again was a job with safety issues, as some of my patients became psychotic and aggressive when off medication or during medication adjustments. After a year at the job, I was attacked by a psychotic patient that went off his medication. I had entered his home to fill his medication box and he came at me with a 2x4 with nails sticking out of it. He chased me over couches and around tables until I was able to escape out the back door. I continued with the job until I was able to find employment elsewhere.

I received a phone call from Max around 7pm which I thought was strange since Alexander and Andrew were with him that evening. In a matter-of-fact tone, Max reported, "Alexander and Andrew were at a neighbor's birthday party and Andrew fell in their pool. They didn't know how long he was laying in the bottom of the pool, but Alexander noticed, jumped in and fished him out. He is fine and back at the party."

I was speechless and once I finally found my words, I responded, "What? They are 4 and 5 years old. Why were they allowed to go to a party, at night, around a pool, without your supervision? It's not a neighbor's responsibility to watch them! And you let them go back!? Go get them right now and bring them home! Is Andrew really okay? Did he lose consciousness?"

Max was agitated and said, "I don't know. All I know is Alexander said he was looking for Andrew, could not find him, looked in the pool and Andrew was at the bottom of the pool not moving, so he jumped in and got him out."

At this point I was frantic. I shouted at Max to hang up, go get them and I would pick them up immediately. He responded, "What's the big deal? He's fine. Whatever, I will go get them."

I added this incident to the ever-growing notebook I kept regarding Max's poor parenting, so if we ended up back in court, I would have the needed documentation.

William continued to struggle with his development. He was not able to speak any words and was getting physically aggressive as he was frustrated with not being able to verbalize what he wants. We developed a way to communicate based on gestures. He was still not taking solid food and would gag and vomit if I attempted to feed him. His pediatrician was still not able to pinpoint the issue and told me to continue working with William and his communication and keep him on a liquid diet.

I was told about an opening in hospice care, an area which I knew nothing about. I was desperate for any other job at this point that I did not have to worry about my safety and if I would be going home to my children at night. I applied and was called in for an interview. Two women sat across from me and asked why I wanted to work for Hospice. My mind started racing. I could lie and say I loved the hospice philosophy and wanted to be a part of it, or I could be honest and say I just want a job that is safe. I went with honesty and thought I could kiss that job prospect goodbye. To my surprise, I received a call two days later with an offer: 5k more a year. I graciously accepted and resigned from my other job. Little did I know that this job would change my life in ways I could not understand.

I completed a two-week orientation for my new position and after my first week, I attended a patient's death with the attending nurse. I was nervous as I traveled out to the home as I had never seen a deceased body that was not already prepared and in a casket at a funeral home. The patient was a beautiful 89-year-old woman that died peacefully in her own bed surrounded by family members. The nurse and I consoled the family, and I called the funeral home to remove the body. As the minutes ticked by, I became increasingly distressed seeing her deceased body lying in bed. I took every measure to conceal my distress from the family, because we were the professionals.

Eventually, the anxiety got the best of me, and I needed to leave the home. I went out to the driveway, got in my car, and bawled my eyes out. Once the nurse was finished, she came outside and over to my car.

She tapped on the window, "What's wrong with you?"

I told her I had never seen a dead body in that manner, and I panicked.

She giggled, and said, "No worries. You will get used to it, promise."

Used to it? How do you get used to that?

I came home that evening and called my father.

"Dad, she was dead. I do not know if I can manage this job. How do you ever get used to something like that? I was supposed to help the nurse prepare the body, and I ran out of the house!"

My father fervently said, "Annie, you need to quit that job. You cannot handle seeing that. Get a nice job that makes you happy."

That was all I needed to hear. I decided at that moment I would stick with that job no matter what it throws my way. I would prove to him and anyone else I could conquer my fear and be successful. I had not come that far to just quit. I had to repeat this to myself daily for the next 5 weeks.

William's pediatrician recommended a wonderful daycare/ educational center for William to attend while I was at work. This center provided speech therapy, occupational therapy, and behavioral therapy with certified professionals. Most of the cost was covered by his insurance, and the rest, I was able to afford.

William spent most of his time at the center in a weighted vest and was given many opportunities for frequent movement. He enjoyed wearing noise canceling headphones to decrease the level of stimulation around him. The center taught him sign language so he could effectively communicate his needs, since he was still unable to speak. I bought videos on sign language and worked with the center's staff to learn it myself. William and I now developed a way of communicating with each other outside of me trying to guess his needs. It was, to me, a small miracle and a gift to be able to now communicate with my son. Still, no insight on a diagnosis; just recommendations for treatment interventions.

Ted finally gave up his pursuit of trying to woo me back and met another woman. She quickly moved in with him and they started building a life together. She was a lovely schoolteacher that was kind and nurturing. I instantly liked her and felt awful for what was to come for her being with Ted. Their relationship started to spiral, and she reached out to me asking to chat. After a period, she looked a shadow of herself- nervous, anxious, depressed, and clearly unsure of herself or her needs. She shared she could not take the abuse anymore and needed to leave. I felt a kinship with her; having weathered the same storm and barely getting out with your sanity.

Weeks later, she moved out of Ted's home and began the long journey of recovery from narcissistic abuse. We stayed in touch throughout the years, and she eventually met and married a loving, supportive man that treated her with the love and respect she deserved. She was a survivor; so was I.

Over the past few years, my alcohol intake waxed and waned. I would stop for periods of time, like during my pregnancy with William, but it would eventually take off again. I attended a few AA meetings, and I was not sure if I was an alcoholic or not. A therapist told me once that if your parent(s) were alcoholics, you are born an alcoholic. Both my parents were alcoholics. Both my mother's parents were alcoholics. I never met my father's parents, but I can assume both his parents were alcoholics too. The genetics regarding alcoholism are so strong, same as any other mental or physical health issue. I took a deep dive into researching alcoholism and searched to define what an alcoholic looks like. I worked full time, got superior performance reviews, cared for and loved my children deeply, provided a clean and safe home, never drank during the day, etc. The picture in my mind of what an alcoholic looked like was the opposite of me - homeless, jobless, childless, hopeless.

I came across an interesting article in one of my favorite psychology magazines looking at alcohol use and abuse. It resonated with me so deeply, that after struggling to define my issue, I decided alcohol was a drug that was impacting me in a negative way. The article did not attempt to define what an alcoholic was, or alcoholism, but addressed problematic drinking. If alcohol is impacting your life in a negative way, whether socially, physically, spiritually, or mentally, then it is time to stop drinking or modify intake. There is a slippery slope. Do you modify it, or stop it altogether?

Some of the diagnostic criteria for diagnosing alcohol abuse and dependency as listed in the Diagnostic and Statistical Manual (DSM) are as follows. Abuse includes recurrent use failing to fulfill major obligations (work, school, home), use despite placing oneself in hazardous conditions (driving drunk), recurrent legal problems, and continued use despite persistent social or interpersonal problems. For dependence criteria: Do you need more alcohol to achieve intoxication? Effects of withdrawal? Desire to decrease intake but unsuccessful? Much time spent obtaining alcohol or recovering from alcohol? Missing important events due to alcohol use? Continued use despite consequences? Other criteria not listed in the DSM includes: Is it difficult to go without alcohol for more than a week? Do you hide your drinking from others?

In contrast to other illnesses or diseases, a diagnosis can be made even if not all criteria are present. So, I met the criteria for dependency, not so much for abuse. Does that mean I was an alcoholic? Did that mean I could no longer drink another alcoholic beverage again for the rest of my life, ever? At that point in my life, yes. Yes, I was an alcoholic and could never drink alcohol again if I wanted to live. Alcoholism is a disease, and with any disease, if not managed, it is life threatening.

I reluctantly confided in a close friend and nurse that I worked with. I knew she was in recovery and was sober for 15+ years. She was regularly active in the AA program and sponsored many in recovery.

"Jody, is there any way to become sober without attending AA meetings?"

The idea that I was different than those that attended AA was a difficult one to wrap my mind around. Jody lovingly took my hand in hers and said, "Annie, no. There is no other way. I will go with you to your first meeting."

I soon thereafter attended my first AA meeting and obtained a sponsor. I grew to see AA is not just a program for those that have had major or life altering consequences in life like homelessness, job loss, time spent in jail or prison, unemployed, etc. It was a program for all walks of life. For lawyers, doctors, mental health therapists, stay at home moms, teachers, politicians, laborers, students, cashiers, etc. I realized through the program that we are all equal as the disease process does not discriminate.

Many in the program approached me after sharing my story saying, "You're fortunate that you caught this disease before it could cause any major issues. You don't have to fall all the way down the well to hit rock bottom."

Sometimes I would go a week, sometimes a month, sometimes numerous months before I would pick up a drink again. Sometimes it was one sip, then starting over again with my sobriety date. Sometimes it was days, and sometimes it was months. Every time I would go back to a meeting and admit my failure to follow the steps and principles. Every 'slip' in sobriety was preceded with the notion that I have licked alcoholism. I had effectively refrained from alcohol for a period of time, so I must not be an alcoholic. I was able to beat the system. I was normal again and could drink like everyone else. That feeling never lasted long.

Inevitably, every relapse was riddled with guilt and shame. This would eventually give way to depression, which led to increased alcohol intake to manage negative feelings. The irony is that it did not *'manage'* negative symptoms, it intensified them. That is the seductive power of alcohol to an alcoholic. It will love you, care for you, always be there for you, numb you, and make you forget all your worries. Somehow, I continued to do well in my job, nurture my children, and maintain friendships. My mental health suffered though. Battling depression and shame was always on the docket. Hiding it from the world felt like a full-time job. In a commercial I remember seeing, a woman hid her true emotions behind a cut out smiley face held in front of her own sad expression. It inspired me to become an expert at disguising my own feelings from the world.

Working at hospice began to feel like wearing a well-worn shoe. I was good at providing care and comfort to my dying patients and their family members. I became the 'go to' for challenging cases. Those patients that had extreme distress with facing death, those patients with young children, those patients that were 'difficult', non-compliant and easily agitated. Others sought my advice for how to work with these issues. It felt good to feel good at what I did.

My role in Hospice was identified as a 'field worker'. I was assigned a caseload of patients, and I was responsible for conducting my visits at their home. Visits included monthly or weekly visits to provide emotional support and education regarding the dying process. I also assisted with helping patients and family members make funeral arrangements, get advanced directives in place, verbalize final wishes, and mend fences with loved ones. Part of this role was to accompany the nurse in the home once the patient died. I assisted the nurse in removing any medical devices from the patient, bathing them, dressing them, calling the funeral home, and providing emotional support to anyone in the home. I considered it sacred work that should be conducted with the utmost dignity and respect. It was an honor to be allowed and present as someone took their last breath. To prepare their body before leaving their earthly home.

The homes we serviced were houses, apartments, mobile homes, hotels, nursing homes, vans, sheds, cars, jails, hospitals, and the woods. Wherever the need was, that is where we went. Somedays I was in a 30-million-dollar mansion on the beach in the morning, and in the afternoon sitting passenger seat in a broken-down van in the woods in 95-degree heat holding the hand of a dying patient demanding to die on their own terms in their own space. I became the advocate for those who wanted to die in the manner they chose. Hospice had a beautiful inpatient facility where patients could go to die in comfort with around the clock care from loving staff. Some staff had extreme difficulty understanding why some would choose to die in a van or in the woods. It was not up to us to decide where the best places a person to die. It WAS up to us to respect and honor the wishes of the dying. Even if it did not match our own wishes.

My firm stance on these ruffled many feathers of coworkers along the way. Some would take their concerns to my supervisor or the CEO in efforts to force me to try and change the wishes of certain patients. Gratefully, I was never asked to change my values regarding this. I often thought what my stance would be if leaders of the organization asked me to do things differently. It was never an option for me to compromise my values, or more especially the wishes of the dying.

Life was so good with my boys. We spent weekends fishing, going to parks, having sleep overs at our home with their friends. We made forts in the house and had pillow fights. We often would all pile into to my bed together every night with bowls of ice cream, watch SpongeBob and have tickle fights. I got Alexander and Andrew involved in flag football, and I so enjoyed watching them play for numerous years, and seeing their self-confidence grow. I marveled at their emerging personalities, their love of nature, their caring and compassion for others, and their resiliency. My children were the light of my life, my reason to get out of bed, my reason to keep going.

Chapter Twelve

'How lucky I am to have something that makes saying goodbye so hard'.
*~ **Winnie The Pooh***

My father was beginning to decline rapidly from stage 4 lung cancer. 52 years of heavy cigarette smoking was finally taking its toll on his health. My half-sister Kip who's living the next town over called me asking for my assistance. Kip and I were not particularly close as she was very jealous of my relationship with our father. She was extremely religious and looked down on those that did not follow what she determined as 'Christian-like'. Me, like most others, were frowned upon. "Annie, you need to convince dad to get chemo and radiation for his cancer. If he does not get it, he will die". It is important to point out that I had already had a heart-to- heart conversation with my father regarding his wishes. He made it extremely clear he would not participate in any life sustaining measures and chemo/radiation were absolutely out of the question. I verbalized to him I would respect those wishes and never push him to do anything he did not want.

"Kip, I will do no such thing. He does not want this, and we need to respect his wishes", I said sternly.

"So, you are okay with him dying. That is how little you care for him?" she seethed.

"Kip, I care for him enough to respect his wishes. There is nothing you can say to change my mind. I suggest you do the same."

With that, she hung up the phone. Wishes aside, I also knew in my heart that there was no amount of chemo and radiation to reverse stage IV advance lung cancer that has already spread to most of his organs and brain.

I had to make the difficult decision to see my father before he died or attend his funeral after because I could not financially manage both. I decided to fly to Indiana to see him and spend a few days helping with his care. He had hospice services through the VA in place and they were a Godsend. He was a particularly stubborn man and insisted dying at home. Only problem was he lived alone and refused any help coming in. Kit did the grocery shopping and helped arrange hospice services. Her total disregard for me during my visit was disgraceful and 'unchristian-like'. Those days with my father were lovely and intimate. He shared pieces of his life he had never shared before. There was one topic off the table - his time in the Korean War. The horror he faced in battle at Inchon was, "not for a daughter's ears to hear."

I longed to know what he saw, and what woke him up screaming in the middle of the night 50 years after being honorably discharged. But I never pushed him to share that.

"Annie, I want you to come over here," he said as he stood at a hutch in the dining room. "In this metal box, I have placed $200 in cash to reimburse you for your airline ticket once I die and you come to my funeral. It will remain in this box with a letter attached to it stating its purpose, so all know it is to be used for this purpose."

My eyes filled with tears knowing I could now afford to come to his funeral. Tears for him worrying about whether I could attend his funeral based on my finances. A final act of love on his part.

We stood in the doorway of his apartment. Me with a suitcase in my hand, and him with his trademark handkerchief in his hand. I reached for his free hand and took it in mine. We both knew this was the last time we would see each other.

How do you say goodbye to the most important person in your life? How do you thank a person for saving your life many times over? How do you part with the one person that gave you unconditional love?

"Annie, you're gonna miss your flight. Go on now," he shifted away from the door.

"Dad, I can't go. I need you."

I immediately felt so selfish for saying this. "Okay dad. I will go. I love you," I swallowed hard.

"Call me what you get home to let me know you made it safe" "I will dad," I said trying to be brave. His hand slipped out from mine, and he turned and shut the door.

And that was the last time I saw my father.

***

Days later, my phone rang at 10pm which jolted me out of bed. I knew at that moment he had died.

"Annie, it's Kit. Dad died. He suffered terribly in the end and was in so much distress," she said flatly.

My heart sank and my stomach came up to my throat. "What? He suffered? Oh God. I will book my flight and a hotel and be there tomorrow."

Her tone changed a bit, "You can stay with me if you want. I will call Linda next, and she will stay here as well."

We ended the call, and I sunk deep into my bed. My life was now forever different. The only one who I could rely on was gone. My best friend.

"No more pain, dad. I love you." I whispered to myself.

Kit was nice enough to send her husband to pick me up from the airport, as I did not have enough funds for a taxi from Chicago's O'Hare airport. I arrived at Kits home and greeted her and Linda. I had not seen Linda since that day we met in the park at the family reunion. Both were very reserved and distant towards me. I felt very unwelcomed but decided I would make the best of it. We had dinner, and I settled in on the couch for the night.

The next morning, we went to dad's home to start clearing out some of his belongings. Kit had already been to the home and removed my father's most precious belongings, all photo albums, important documents, and keepsakes. Kit's adult children were there and starting to empty out his belongings and furniture. His things and furniture were being thrown over the balcony railing and onto the ground to be dragged to the dumpster.

"This is so disrespectful! Why are his things being treated in this way and thrown away?" I barked.

"Annie, what do you expect we do with it? You want to take it home with you?"

I was angry enough the claw her eyes out.

"I expect it be treated with dignity and respect and not thrown over a balcony into the snow."

Kit then pulled out my fathers will from the hutch in the dining room. The same place he placed the funds for my return flight home. "I will read this later and not until I am ready," she boasted.

I went to retrieve the designated envelope with my funds, and it was gone. The box was empty. I asked Kit, "Where is the envelope dad left for me? He specifically left it here for me," I questioned.

"Gee Annie. I don't know what you are talking about", she said with a glint in her eye.

"You stole it, Kit. How Christian-like of you."

At that moment I hated her. I hated her hypocrisy.

That evening, my best friend, Margaret who I worked with at hospice called to check on me. I sobbed as I told her how painful this whole experience had been, and how much I wanted to get through the next couple days. I shared how Kit stole the funds to pay for my plane ticket home which would leave me short for next month's rent. She always knew the right thing to say; her empathy, compassion and friendship was such a blessing to me.

The more time I spent with Margaret, the more I liked her, and the feeling was mutual.

"Annie, I have to say, Kit painted an awful picture of you before you arrived, but I couldn't tell she was lying to me," Linda shared.

We both agreed that we wanted to get to know each other better. It was a bright spot in this time of gut-wrenching grief.

The viewing and funeral felt surreal. I wrote a letter to my father while on the plane and placed it in a small wooden box. I tucked in in his casket as I said my final goodbyes. More people came to the funeral than I had anticipated. There were veterans that served with him in the Korean War there to pay final respects. A few approached me while I stood at his casket and shared memories of my father. They also shared some of the horrors they witnessed while in battle. I learned some of the things my that father said should *never be heard by a daughter's ear*. I wish I had not been told, as some things should be left unsaid.

Standing over the open grave while my father was being lowered into the ground was almost more than I could bare. The bitter frigid wind cut through my clothing and into my core. Snow pelted the side of the casket draped in the American flag. The flower petals on top seemed to shiver from the blistering wind. I could not stand the thought of him being placed in the cold freezing ground, exposed to the elements. At that moment, life felt too cruel, so merciless, so final.

Kit had previously stated she would drive me back to the airport in Chicago for my return flight home. A couple hours before I was to leave, Kit stated, "You will need to find your own ride to Chicago. I don't want to be bothered with it."

She took such joy in expressing this, knowing I had no car, no money for a taxi. I reached out to another family member that attended the funeral, and they happily offered to drive me. I vowed at that moment, my relationship with Kit was over and it could never be repaired.

On the plane home, I wrote a thank you letter to the family member that drove me to the airport. I then pulled out a new journal and wrote all the happy memories and sayings my father often said to me; the greetings we had for each other, the funny euphemisms and banter. I know how the memory fades and little bits and pieces are lost. I wanted to remember it always. I gazed out the plane window and watched the puffy white clouds below illuminated orange and red by the setting sun. Thoughts about my plane ride to Indiana before my senior year in high school, listening to U2, and anxious to start my new life with my father. Now was a new life without my father. *'I love you dad'*, I whispered as I imagined seeing him dancing in the clouds with Brutus.

That night, I crawled into bed and felt a depth so lonely I wondered if I would ever feel joy again. Tears streamed down my face, and I clung tightly to my pillow. I then heard the TV in the living room click on. I got up from bed and stood in the living room looking around. The kids were asleep in their beds, no one was up. I clicked it off, not thinking much of it and got back into bed. A minute later, the TV clicked on again. What in the world is going on? I got up again, looked around, no one. My nerves were jangled at this point, and I could feel the hair on the back of my neck stand up. I flipped off the TV and got back into bed. Please, I just need some sleep. And with that thought, the TV clicked on again. I screamed from the top of my lungs, "Stop it! Stop it! I know it is you dad. I cannot deal with this. Please, just stop!" And with that, the TV clicked off and it was silent the rest of the night.

I arrived at work the next morning to cards, flowers, and homemade snacks on my desk in my cubicle. Tears flowed down my faces as my coworkers greeted me home and expressed their sympathies. I opened the first card, and in it was $200. The card read, 'We are family, and you are an important piece. Just a gift to cover your rent. Love Always'. I sat in shock as to the love, compassion, and generosity of my work family. I felt truly blessed.

It's strange how grief works. It is like you are standing still and the rest of the world keeps going. How is it that the rest of the world is just going about their business when my world is in such disarray? The brain feels fuzzy, and things feel like they move in slow motion. Movement requires more energy, and the senses feel heightened. You become very acquainted with the pit in your stomach. The ache that is hard to put into words. A mix between pain, nausea, and flip-flopping. People say it will pass and it will get better; just be patient. That is the thing with grief, it does not pass, you just learn how to live with it.

It reminded me of my favorite quote by Elizabeth Kubler- Ross - '*The reality is that you will grieve forever. You will not get over the loss of a loved one; you will learn to live with it. You will heal and you will rebuild yourself around the loss you have suffered. You will be whole again, but you will never be the same. Nor should you be the same nor would you want to*'.

Many beautiful moments came out of the grief of watching people die. One moment I will carry with me forever was the day I showed up at my female patient's home and was standing at the front door waiting for the caregiver to let me in. At my feet was a tiny sparrow tapping at the glass pane that ran alongside the front door. Tap tap tap.

He steadily and gently tapped on the glass and was not fazed at all by me standing inches from him. The son inevitably answered the door and let me in. He looked frazzled, exhausted, and bewildered as he plopped down on the couch facing the front door. I sat beside him and began talking softly. He said, "I didn't tell you, but my dad died unexpectedly yesterday. The grief of watching my mom die was too much for him. As soon as he died, that sparrow, as he pointed to the front door, landed there, and started tapping on the glass. He has not moved from that spot in 24 hours. It's my dad waiting for his wife to come home to him in heaven." We sat side by side for what felt like eternity, staring at the sparrow tapping at the glass and peering in through the window.

Days later I received a phone call from the son stating his mom had just died. I told him me and the nurse would be right out, and we hurried right over. I knocked at the front door and the sparrow was gone. The son answered the door and said, "he just left. The sparrow, my dad, left as soon as my mom took her last breath." A faint hint of a smile came over his face and said, they are both home now, home together.

Chapter Thirteen

"The bad news is time flies. The good news is you're the pilot."

~ ***Michael Altshuler***

Months passed, and Max called when Christmas was approaching. He asked what I was planning to buy the boys for Christmas as he did not want to duplicate my presents. I told him the boys wanted their first video game system, and I was going to purchase this for them. He acknowledged this and let me know what he was purchasing. I was so excited for Christmas morning to see the joy on their face opening this gift I spent nine months saving for. Eight days before Christmas, the boys came back from being with Max for two days and they have never been so excited. They screamed mom you won't believe this dad bought us our first video game system and we have been playing it for two days straight I can't wait to go back there. My heart just shattered. How could he do this? I waited for the kids to go to bed, and I called Max, hands trembling as I dialed the phone. "How dare you! I told you I had saved for months for this and was going to give them this for Christmas!"

He laughed and said, "Oh well. Now they have one here too.

Merry Christmas."

When Max and I divorced, and I separated from Ted, I made a solum promise to myself that I would never speak poorly about Max or Ted in front of the children. I knew the horrible damage it did to me hearing my mother constantly speak poorly of my father. I was the go between. So much so, I never saw my parents in the same room together until my wedding day. I honored this and kept my promise despite the much-needed tongue biting that occurred quite often.

When Alexander turned ten years-old, my mother stated she would like to take me, Alexander and Andrew on a 4-day cruise to the Bahamas. "Moving forward", she said, "I plan to do a nice trip for each grandkid on their tenth birthday." As with many offered gifts from my mother, many never came to fruition, so I set my expectations low for these proposed trips.

To my surprise, the trip was booked and one month later we headed off to Miami to board a beautiful cruise liner. Unfortunately, the cruise coincided with a tropical storm that followed us the duration of the trip. We made the best of it, as the kids had the entire pool to themselves, ate unlimited ice cream and ordered cheeseburgers and soda via room service before bed. Mid trip, while the boys played in the video arcade room, my mother sat down in a chair poolside and stated, "Annie, I need to tell you something. It's a bit embarrassing, but it is important you know." I said across from her, as the band of rain from the tropical storm started to pass. She shifted uncomfortably before saying "I had an affair during my first marriage to your sisters' father. During that affair I became pregnant with your sister Louise, and never told a soul. The marriage was falling apart, and I needed love. Louise's father thinks he is the biological father to Louise, and Louise is unaware."

Everything froze in time for me as I tried to wrap my mind around what I just heard. 'What? Not her real father? Why is she telling me this? Why does Louise not know? Is this real?' So many questions ran through my mind as my mother stared waiting for me to respond. I uttered, "Why are you telling me this?" Her discomfort turned to joy, obvious by the glint in her eye and the smirk on her face. I knew the look well. It is what I saw right before she swung the leather belt taking out all her rage on my body. She responded, "Well, you know Louise was always so mean to you growing up, and you never fought back as she was so much older than you. You now have a weapon to use against her. You now can hurt her and cut her to the core." I raised my hand and shouted, "I don't want to hear anymore. This is absurd. I can't believe you are even telling me this." She looked horrified that I would look a gift horse in the mouth. "Annie, I am handing you the weapon, you just need to use it. I just have one demand. You must wait until I am dead before sharing this. Not that I care what she thinks of me, but the one she thinks is her real father is dead, and once I am dead, the identity of her real father dies with me. She will never be able to find her biological father. That will be the ultimate revenge for you! Isn't that great?!"

I jumped up from the chair and paced the pool deck. The next weather band was quickly approaching, and my head was swirling and my stomach was lurching. Anger replaced dismay as I ran up to her, squatted down to meet her eye level and said, "I will never hurt my sister like this. I will never be you. I hope you rot in Hell." With that, I spun on my heel and raced to the video room to find the boys. "Look mom!", exclaimed Andrew. "Aren't these arcade games so cool!? I love Grammy so much for bringing us here." My confused brain could barely make out what he said, as my knees shook, and my stomach rose to my throat. "Yes sweetheart, it's so cool." I slipped away to the corner of the small arcade room to escape the flashing lights, and kids screaming so I could further process what I just heard.

'Why did I agree to come here? Why didn't I expect she would do or say something hurtful? How could I be so stupid?' The questions came rapid fire, but with them, no answers. Just pain, sadness and guilt. The question as to whether to share this with Louise or not would haunt me for years to come. *'Doesn't she have the right to know? Would I want to know? Is my father truly my father? She did tell me before boarding that plane at 17 years old that he may not be. Was that true? He is dead now and I may never know, and I can't trust a word that falls out of her retched mouth.'* I snapped back to the present when I heard my mother's voice. "Are you having fun Alexander? Don't you just have the best Grammy ever to bring you here for your birthday?" Her eyes then met

mine from across the room and she mouthed the words, "I love you".

The next year, I met Tony, the man that would become my husband. We dated on and off for a couple of years, until we committed to each other in 2009. He was never married previously and had no children of his own. I was baffled that he chose to be with me. A divorced mom of three boys aged 12, 11, and 7. He loved me for me, and he fell in love with my boys. For ten years I was a single mom and refused to settle for anyone that did not treat me and my children with the love and respect we deserved. Their stability and happiness were paramount, and now I could have both.

At 70 years old, my mom received the diagnosis of Parkinson's Disease. Her verbalization of the disease was one of quick decline, then a painful death. Not knowing much about Parkinson's Disease at the time of her diagnosis, I did extensive research on this diagnosis. After doing so, I sat her down and shared with her my findings.

"Mom, I have learned that those diagnosed with Parkinson's can continue to have a happy and productive life for many years after diagnosis. The progression is typically slow."

She became irritated and stated, "You kids just live in fantasy land and don't care what is happening to me."

She went on to say, "No one believes that Parkinson's is a devastating, fatal disease and that I am over-exaggerating my illness."

I felt very torn between wanting to validate her emotions, and yelling, "You always over exaggerate any and every malady you have ever had, so it makes it hard to believe anything that comes out of your mouth!"

Instead, I whispered, "I'm sorry mom. I believe you and love you."

I reached over to hug her, and her touch was ice cold.

"Annie, I had so many kids so I could get the love I never received as a child, but I am still not loved. None of you love me."

My heart broke for her. I loved her. I wanted nothing but love from her. It's hard to love your abuser, but I did.

***

The next few years of my mother's life consisted of traveling, gardening, and photography. She was active and took photography lessons from the well revered photographer, Clyde Butcher. He was famous for his beautiful black and white photos of cypress swamps in the Everglades National Park. She shared with me her adventures of trekking through the swamps with Clyde and photographing alligators and snakes while in waist deep water. Her eyes lit up when recalling the excitement and beauty of the wildlife and raw nature of the swamps.

Her passion for photography sparked mine. I did not have the time, raising three boys as a single mom to learn the art of photography, but I knew someday I would. A few years before, I had bought a cheap camera of my own and went out photographing trees while visiting my father up north. I anxiously awaited the three days waiting for them to be developed at the local Walgreens. Once back, I flipped through them with pure joy. I had picked out the best couple of photos and excitedly showed them to mom once I returned home. I watched her face as she gazed at the photos.

"So, what do you think?" I was bursting inside waiting for her words of praise.

She tossed them onto the coffee table and with disinterest

said, "They are not that good."

Not that good? Well, they are not as good as hers, but it was my first time trying my hand at photography. My mouth hung open as she strolled into the kitchen and started making coffee. I didn't take another photo of nature for the next 14 years.

I received a phone call from my mother stating her blood pressure was extremely high and a friend said she needs to go to the emergency room. For years, she was preoccupied with monitoring her blood pressure numerous times a day. Never had there ever been an issue with her blood pressure in the past.

"Well, what is your blood pressure?"

She responded, "210 over 130," as she slurred her words.

I grabbed my keys and ran out of the house. We lived two streets apart, so I was there in two minutes. I put her in the car and rushed to the closest hospital. She was stabilized and admitted for observation. The attending physician stated the stroke was most likely due to the new medication she was recently prescribed. He stated he will confer with her primary physician.

Her primary physician was kind enough to visit my mother in the hospital and examine her.

"I understand the medication I prescribed was what most likely elevated your blood pressure to the point that you had a stroke. I will write an order in your chart discontinuing the medication."

She held my mother's hand and told her she was going to be fine.

I sat with her for most of the day until I had to pick the kids up from school.

"Mom, I need to get the kids, but I will be back in a couple hours."

She squeezed my hands and left her side. Two hours later, as I was preparing to go back to the hospital, I received a call from my mother stating she didn't feel well, and something was wrong.

I hurried back to the hospital, and I was not allowed in the room, as the nurses were working quickly to stabilize her again. I spoke to the head nurse at the nurse's station, asking what had happened.

"It appears she has had another stroke."

Another stroke? She was fine when I left. "Did she receive

any kind of treatment while I was gone?" I asked.

"Well, she was given her medication as ordered. That was it."

I felt irritated and that something was amiss. I asked to see her chart.

"Her chart?" the nurse looked suspiciously at me.

"Yes, her chart. I am her health care surrogate, and I want to see it now."

She slammed the chart hard on the countertop and hovered as I leafed through it until I reached the section on medication orders. I have scanned enough medical charts working with hospice and in psychiatric units, that I knew exactly where to look. My eyes grew big, and my stomach flipped in my belly.

"Her primary physician wrote an order for continuation of the medication that caused her stroke. She was just here two hours ago and said she will write an order to discontinue it."

The nurse spun the chart around and gazed at the newly written order.

"Did you give that medication to her while I was gone?" I barked.

She shifted nervously, "Well, yes. I followed the doctor's order and gave the medication." I saw red.

"I want to see the hospitalist, and I do not give permission for her primary doctor to ever step foot in her room or touch her chart ever again!"

Other nurses in the station stopped what they were doing, spun around in their chairs, and watched the drama unfold as I stood screaming orders at the poor nurse standing in front of me.

"I will stand here until you tape a big note on the front of her chart that her primary, who is now fired from the case, is not allowed to 'treat' my mother."

I could tell she was torn between wanting to tell me off for being demanding to feeling empathetic to what just happened.

I sat bedside with my mother until she was discharged, as the guilt from leaving her side before led to another stroke.

"Annie, you know all patients need an advocate sitting vigil while in the hospital. They will kill you if someone doesn't question every pill given and every treatment administered."

I knew this was her typical over-exaggeration, but after what she just went through, I could appreciate her statement.

A year and a half earlier, I had a hysterectomy due to cervical cancer cells in the same hospital. I had just been transferred from the recovery room to the room I would be staying in for a couple days when the nurse came in, scanned my plastic bracelet, and handed me a pill.

"Here's some water, swallow that down honey", in her southern drawl.

Even in my medicated haze, I thought to myself, pill?

What pill?

"What medication is it?" I asked.

"It's the medication your doctor ordered. Just take it," now getting irritated.

"I'm not taking a damn pill unless I know what it is!" I bellowed.

She matched my tone, "It's for your blood pressure. You know, the medication you have been on since before you had surgery!"

Blood pressure? I didn't have issues with blood pressure. She was again fiddling with my plastic bracelet. I yanked my arm away and looked at the bracelet. 'Janet Smith'. Who is Janet Smith?

The realization of what was going on, started to penetrate my hazing mind. "You have the wrong identification bracelet on me. I'm not Janet Smith. I am Annie Williams."

The nurse turned white as a sheet, plucked the medication from my fingers, spun around on her heels, and left the room. A minute later she returned and cut the bracelet off my wrist and quickly again left the room.

Why on God's green earth did I question this one action after having such blind faith in every other action that had taken place that day? I looked up to the ceiling, "Thank you."

In 2009, what started as a pain in the right side of my stomach, increasingly grew to an absolute pain in the neck came and go at will. After numerous trips to the emergency room, different doctors, every test known to man, a physician finally looked at me and said, "Have you ever considered this is all in your head?"

I was so angry, scared, and losing weight rapidly as I could not eat without horrible pain.

My primary physician reluctantly said, "Well I can refer you to a surgeon, but you know what surgeons like to do; operate. Maybe they can open you up and see what's going on."

I emphatically accepted this offer and scheduled surgery. The surgeon left the operating room and told my soon to be husband that my gallbladder had ruptured and looked like a black deflated balloon.

He went on to say how lucky I was to have not and septic and survived.

Once recovered, I gladly wrote a contemptuous letter to the physician that asked me to consider if this was all in my head.

Chapter Fourteen

"Family dysfunction rolls down from generation to generation, like a fire in the woods, taking down everything in its path until one person in one generation has the courage to turn and face the flames. That person brings peace to their ancestors and spares the children that follow."

~ ***Terry Real***

In the early spring of 2010, Tony proposed to me. It was an incredibly special and endearing moment in my life. He shared with me how much he loved the boys and how blessed he felt to have a family, outside of his family of origin that loved him. I knew he was sent to me by my father, and it happened at just the right time in my life. A time I was ready to share my life with someone who was healthy, loving, and strong.

We shared the joyous news with family and friends, and they all gave us their best wishes. Tony's parents treated me as their own daughter and my children as their grandchildren. I felt so incredibly grateful to be welcomed into such a loving family.

Tony and I completed our wedding invitations and my mother requested certain people she would like to invite. We happily agreed to have those she wished attend. Among them, was her cousins, Bob, and Jeanne. She asked us not to send a formal invitation to them, but she would create an email that she requested I proofread before she sent it. I thought it was odd for her to request this, but I obliged.

Days later, I came to her home and said I would be happy to proofread her email now. She became very nervous, could not make eye contact, and stated, "It's okay, I already sent it to them." I questioned why she seemed so nervous and what was said in the email. She fumbled through her words but expressed that she invited them and would let me know what they say.

I have very fond memories of Bob and Jeanne. We spent many holidays together and they always treated me with such kindness. I knew deep in my heart, my mother's email to them was filled with lies and distain for my happiness. I decided to do something I was not very proud of, but I accessed her email once I returned home. She had recently given me her login and password to do some work on her computer.

The email sent to Bob and Jeanne was indeed not an invitation, but two-page tirade about her dislike for my fiancé's parents, our plans for an 'over-the-wall, tacky' wedding, which was so uncouth for a woman's second marriage, and how our expectation for her to foot the bill for the wedding was atrocious. My head spun as I read the words that seemed to spill off the paper with such vitrail.

She ended her email begging them not to attend the *three-* ringed circus and to say a prayer for their, "broke and saddened cousin that had to sell the family silver to pay for a wedding while she lives below the poverty line."

My stomach surged up to my throat as I had to hold back my dinner. My shock quickly turned to rage, and I picked up the phone and dialed her number.

She answered the phone, "Hi Lovie."

I was seething inside as I paced the living room with the phone crushed against my ear. "How dare you! How dare you write such lies to Bob and Joanne and portray me and my fiancé in such an untruthful and hurtful manner. We haven't asked for a single penny! You said you wanted to pay flowers and a cake and was gratefully accepted."

Years of anger and frustration came spilling out of mouth and into her ears. "Poverty line? You soaked all four husbands for every penny they had."

I continued "Why can't you just be happy for me? Why do you have to cause so much pain? Why can't you just love me and treat me with kindness?"

She was stunned. She denied writing it and sending it. The gaslighting was in full force and the ace securely kept in her back pocket, just to be pulled at times like this.

"I saw their response. I saw their sympathy towards you. I saw they declined to attend as they did not want to take part in such a disgusting event that has hurt their loving cousin, my poverty- stricken mother, so deeply."

I told her not to come. I told her we no longer accepted her gift to pay for flowers and a cake. If she was so against this marriage and ceremony she was not welcomed. Her gaslighting turned to tears and apathy for herself. Our call ended, and I fully expected her to kill herself. She had threatened this in the past and used it as a weapon to gain my forgiveness. This would be something she would do just to spite me and punish me.

A few hours passed and my guilt became center stage.

'What if she did kill herself? Could I live with that?' I thought to myself as I continued pacing. I dialed her number, and she answered in a voice that sounded like a remorseful little girl. "Mom don't even think of killing yourself. If you have any love for me, you will not do that."

She whispered, "Fine." "You promise?" I asked.

"Yes, I promise." With that I hung up.

From that moment forward, she convinced herself my fiancé put me up to making that phone call and that he was actively driving a wedge in our relationship. Her love for him turned to distain, and she would let everyone in her life know exactly what she thought about him. She told family and friends he was in the mafia, and he planned to kill his father. He was a dangerous man, and silly Annie was throwing away her life and loving relationship with her mother to a man that was a monster.

Weeks later, mom announced that she took the email she wrote to Bob and Joanne to her therapy session, and her therapist stated, "There was nothing in that email that was hurtful."

I told her she was delusional, and her therapist was obviously delusional. I knew it was a lie and had no interest in challenging her any longer on the subject. Her lies became her reality, and that reality was unshakable. She later shared with me that her therapist then diagnosed her with bipolar disorder.

Maybe her therapist wasn't delusional after all.

***

Tony and I married in 2011 on his sailboat docked at a beautiful yacht club surrounded by family and friends. The day was delightful. Not a cloud in the crystal blue sky. At the helm was my sister, Sandy standing next to me as my maid of honor and Tony's father at his side as his best man. My beautiful three sons walked me down the aisle. The chaplain I worked with at hospice officiated the ceremony. As Tony held my hands in his, I knew that I would love him until the day I died. He was my best friend, my confidant and now my husband.

2013 brought with it a new medical malady for me. Again, stomach pain, nausea, pain with eating. Again, numerous doctor visits, testing, no answers. What started as mild symptoms, grew into not being able to pass solid food from my stomach to small intestines. I lived off shakes and baby food with my weight plummeting. I began to think I was going to die and leave behind my husband and three children. Finally, I received a phone call from my doctor's office with blood results.

The nurse stated, "You have Celiac disease."

"What? What is Celiac disease?" I asked.

She responded, "Just don't eat gluten and follow up with a nutritionist."

What's gluten? And with that she hung up.

Needless to say, Google became my best friend and I educated myself extensively on Celiac disease and how to manage it. The good news was that it could be treated by diet modification. But non-adherence could lead to digestive cancers and death.

I have a whole new appreciation for those with food allergies because of this diagnosis. I was unfortunately diagnosed during a time when gluten free was a fad many followed, and looked upon as a dietary choice, not a mandate. Good news, there was a lot of gluten free choices and food products. Eating out became challenging, as many wait staff, when asked if the food was gluten-free, would just roll their eyes and respond, "I think so." Eating became scary for me. What is safe? What isn't? Reading every food label in the grocery store scanning for gluten before feeling comfortable enough to put it in my cart. I eventually gravitated towards simple, whole foods: chicken, fish, fruits, vegetable, nuts, and no longer eating packaged foods as those often have hidden glutens. It took months to feel 'normal' again when it came to eating. In the end, I am grateful for the diagnosis versus what my brain imagined it could be.

In 2015, Alexander was graduating high school, and we discussed his thoughts on college and his future education. He decided on a local college, and I assisted him in jumping through all the hoops of the enrollment period. I called Max to let him know Alexander needed the funds Max told me he socked away in a prepaid college fund instead of paying child support all those years.

Max said, "College fund? He doesn't have a college fund. What are you talking about?"

It felt like I had been punched in the stomach.

"You told me years ago you were putting money in savings for the kid's college tuition. That's why I never enforced child support payments!"

He laughed and replied, "I never said that. They will have to figure it out for themselves."

What a sucker I was. There was never any intention to save money for them, just hurt me and make life more difficult.

William's pediatrician gave Tony and I a referral to the Miami Children's Hospital for a neurological workup to further assess William's hyperactivity, aggression and difficulty learning. Through this assessment, William was diagnosed with ADHD and started on medication to assist him with his disruptive behaviors and attention. The drug felt like a miracle. His ability to sit still in class and focus on learning improved drastically. It was an incredible relief to finally start getting some answers to his behaviors, and guidance to better meet his needs.

As time passed, William's school became move involved and began psychological and IQ testing to assess for intellectual disabilities and established an Individual Educational Plan. It was determined by the psychologist that William had a significant learning disability with a borderline IQ of 70. At this time, it was decided to put William in specialized classes that would be tailored to his educational needs. Teachers finally started seeing William as a child with disabilities instead of a child that was defiant and difficult.

Seven years after receiving her diagnosis of Parkinson's Disease, my mother's abdomen was growing to the point of much concern. Her diet was awful and consisted of mostly carrot cake and ice cream, but the weight gain was rapid. After numerous doctor appointments over a three-month period, she was finally diagnosed with Stage 3 Ovarian Cancer. Having worked in hospice for 10 years at that point, I knew at the time this was a death sentence for her. She told us immediately she didn't want Chemo or radiation as her body could not handle the toxic effects of this treatment.

"I just want to live, whatever time I have left feeling good." "I will respect whatever your wishes are."

I offered for her to meet with the medical director at hospice to answer whatever questions or concerns she may have regarding her diagnosis and prognosis. We had worked together for many years and had become close friends. I asked him to come to her home and provide education and support; he happily did so. After his visit, mom felt certain she was making the right decision regarding no aggressive treatment.

After a couple months, mom became so uncomfortable with her growing belly. It pressed against her lungs, and she became short of breath. The discomfort in her pelvis was almost intolerable. She connected with a Gynecological Oncologist surgeon that recommended removal of the tumor load, debulking, to provide comfort from pain and pressure.

"Annie, this is a no-brainer. I can't live like this anymore."

The surgery was scheduled for three weeks. In the meantime, mom got a nasty cold, and there was much debate as to whether she should have the surgery being sick. The surgeon stated we must move forward despite the small risk of her not surviving the surgery. The day came and she was getting prepped for surgery.

"Annie, I love you. I always have. If I don't wake up, I have had a full life."

Tears filled my eyes as we said our good-byes.

"I will be here when you wake up," and with that, she was wheeled into surgery.

The hours ticked by slowly until the surgeon walked into the waiting area. It seemed like eternity for him to reach the area where I was sitting. My legs were too wobbly to stand and walk to him.

"She did well and is in recovery. You may see her soon."

The slow process of recovery began as she arrived home with private duty care. The next few weeks were filled with pain, tears and then relief. During this journey, she walked out of her bathroom and into her bedroom where I was standing and was sobbing. She lifted her nightgown and exposed her belly.

"Look at what he did to me! He sliced me from sternum to pelvis and did a shitty job sewing me up!"

The scar to me was nicely healing and most of the bulk was now gone. "Mom, you had major surgery, and this measure probably has probably prolonged your life and created comfort."

Now hysterical, "You don't get it! I am not longer attractive. He stole my vanity!"

I tried very hard to understand and be compassionate, but my brain had a difficult time processing her statements. She is alive! She is comfortable. She should be grateful! "I'm sorry mom. I love you."

The surgery gave her hope, and later decided to do chemotherapy per the surgeon's recommendation. He referred us to see an oncologist of our choosing to oversee her treatment. I knew most of the oncologists in town, and picked the one that had the best reputation. Juggling her doctor appointments, my work schedule and the kids was challenging to say the least. The stress was building, and my mother's dependency on me to help her make medical decisions was becoming overwhelming.

She often asked me questions about death. What was it like to die? Would she suffer? Was there really a Heaven? Would my parents be happy to see me or reject me again? I had heard these questions hundreds of times working in hospice, but never by my mother.

The gravity I felt placed on my shoulders was almost more that I could bare. I was caught between the daughter who works in the medical field and is helping make medical decisions, the daughter who was just a daughter, and the daughter of a mother that was cruelly abusive and borderline sadistic in her treatment and behavior. The emotions between guilt, love, anger, sorrow, grief, and relief were like a boxer in a ring with numerous opponents. Which emotion would win today? This hour? This moment? The ability to be fully present at work and at home was increasingly difficult.

Sitting in the waiting room with my mother for her appointments with the oncologist was depressing at best. She sat next to me with a scarf wrapped around her bald head. She and I watched other patients arrive and others leave, equally frail, pasty in color with a lost look in their eyes. The medicinal smell, the sterile feel, the nervous anticipation. The chemotherapy was taking a toll on mom and her cancer continued to grow and spread despite this. It spread to her brain, as her cognitive ability started to decline. The spread to the brain was not formally diagnosed, but it was obvious considering the normal course of the disease process and her cognition.

At the conclusion of one doctor appointment, the physician whispered in my ear and walked out of the room. He had asked me to follow him, and I did.

"Annie, you work in the field of death and dying. She is dying and the chemo is speeding it along. She needs to stop the chemo, and you are the best one to tell her." And with that, he walked away.

"Wait, what? I need to tell her?" He turned the corner his office and shut the door. I stood at the entryway, facing the closed door to the office she sat in, for what felt like forever. This was the beginning of the end, and I had to tell her. How do I tell her? The brief anticipation of doing so was worse than any anticipation I ever felt waiting for her to enter my bedroom and administer a beating.

I took a deep breath, opened the door and said, "Come on mom, we are going home."

She looked confused but follow suit. We got in the car, and I hesitated to turn the ignition.

"Annie, it's over, isn't it?"

I began to tremble. "Mom, he said the chemo isn't helping anymore and we need to stop."

She stared blankly, "Why didn't he tell me that?"

Such a great question. "I don't know mom. Maybe he thought it would be easier coming from me."

She sat for a few minutes, just gazing out the window as I scanned her face trying to decipher what she was thinking. "Okay, let's go home."

I hated him at that moment. How could he put me in this position? How could I allow him to put me in this position? What a coward. That was the end of our visits with him.

The doctor I worked with often checked in with me and inquired how mom was doing. He was a compass for me through this journey. He guided me as to what to expect, prognosis, and comfort measures. Nothing like being on the other side of the fence when it's your own family member. The newly acquired empathy I now had for those navigating the disease process had strengthened exponentially. The compassion and empathy were always there, but now it was so close I could feel it in my core. The desperation, the unknown and the fear.

For my mother's 78th birthday, her three daughters decided to take her away for the weekend to a vacation rental at the beach. The two-story stilt beach home sat on the Gulf in beautiful Ft Myers beach. My three boys, Louise's three girls, and Sandy's two sons and daughter accompanied as well to enjoy in the festivities. The home was a perfect location to relax, enjoy the warm Gulf waters and the large pool surrounded by lush, tropical foliage. I think we all knew it was the last time we would ever be on vacation with our mother, and all together as a family. It was bittersweet.

Me, my mother and two sisters waded out into the Gulf with our pool noodles in hand. We made idle chit chat as we floated in a circle.

Mom got a tear in her eye and said, "You have to promise me something." We fell silent and waited in anticipation. "Once I die, please stick together. Love each other. You need to promise me this."

We were quick to agree, but with it, some feelings of reservation. She spent years tearing us down, pitting us against each other, talking poorly about us to each other, and spreading lies to keep us apart. I suppose it was self-preservation on her part to do so. If we came in alliance, she would lose control over us. The dynamics would change, and she would suffer another loss.

The anger seared through me as I contemplated her request. How dare she ask such a thing? How dare she place this expectation on us after all these years. The discomfort was obvious, yet we acknowledged her request. The subject changed and the moment was over.

The day came we needed to take the car keys away. She had driven to the grocery store a mile away and got lost coming home. She called me from the side of the road, and she said nothing looked familiar. I found her and brought her home. Me and my two sisters met her at her home to discuss no longer driving. We all knew it was going to be a contemptuous conversation and she would not give in easily. We all stated our case as to why we felt this would be the best decision for all of us and she looked each of us squarely in the eyes and said, "Fuck you. Fuck you. And fuck you. You will have to dig the keys out of my cold dead hands before I will ever hand them over to any of you." Well, that went as expected.

Later that day, she finally handed them over, though not without a few more words of frustration directed towards us. The car remained in the garage unless the private duty caregiver took her grocery shopping or for ice cream.

My career with Hospice was taking off. I had climbed up the ladder from field worker to supervisor, to manager, and now director. I loved my job and I felt good at it. I mentored others and provided supervision to therapists seeking licensure. I quickly learned you either fell in love with working for Hospice or found out it was not for you. I sat with hundreds of patients as they took their last breath. I held dozens of sobbing family members as they watched their loved ones be taken out by a Funeral Home. I held the hands of young mothers as they said goodbye to their children dying of cancer. I gently and lovingly bathed and dressed dozens of deceased patients, so their loved ones come to the room to say their last goodbye before leaving their homes.

One death especially touched me in a way I will never forget. A 50 something year old man was sitting vigil as his 20 something year old son was actively dying. Hospice volunteers frequently made beautiful quilts that adorned each bed in the inpatient unit. This young man had a colorful twin size quilt with yellow butterflies all over it covering his failing body. His father half-heartedly chuckled and said, "he's such a tough guy. He went through the army and fought in Afghanistan. If he only knew he had a quilt with butterflies all over, he would be so angry with me." Moments later his son gave in to death and his father let go of his hand and walked over to the window and efforts to hide his tears. I helped the nurse prepare his body and lay a rose on his bedside table as we always did. I looked up to check on the grieving father and his mouth was gaping open staring out the window in amazement. I walked over and looked out to see what he may be staring at, and right outside the window was a huge, fluttering storm of yellow butterflies dancing and fluttering around. We both stood there side by side. His hand reached over and met mine and we were frozen watching this beautiful miracle in front of our eyes.

I visited my mother almost daily. I came to her home on a Saturday and could hear voices coming from her bedroom. The private duty caregiver was giving mom a shower and mom was talking loud over the flow of the water.

"Well, just wait until I die. I'm gonna have the last laugh. She thinks she could choose her new husband over me and get away with it. I wish I could be a fly on the wall to see her reaction. It will be epic."

My heart sank knowing she was talking about me. The rage and jealousy she felt after I married my husband was toxic. She lost any control she thought she had over me the day I married him. She was going to make me pay for this betrayal, and she did.

For years, she said she planned to leave her home to me and most of her savings. This was always uncomfortable to hear, as talking about her eventual death was painful.

"Annie, the girls have plenty of money and they will inherit so much money once their father's wife dies. Your brother was never there for me, and I don't want him to have anything. I want my money to go to you and the boys to insure your financial stability. I have already drawn it up in my will and it's done."

I knew this would create a strained dynamic between me and my siblings but was not that concerned.

My mother felt betrayed by me when I married my husband, and after the prompting of a sibling, the Will changed. Everything would be divided equally. Another punishment and promise not fulfilled. I did not allow this to sway my care and concern for her. I continued showing up daily, loving her, caring for her and being the person I wished she had been for me; unconditionally.

Hospice was now involved, and I hand-picked her team of hospice providers. She had the best of the best. They visited often and kept the family up to date on her condition. The nurse and social worker were in with mom while Sandy and I waited in the living room. We tried to always respect her privacy when with caregivers.

We overheard mom say, "I know Annie wants to stick me in a nursing home. She's a selfish bitch and never really loved me."

Something inside of me snapped. Here were my peers, that I respected in with my mother as she talked poorly about me. What a humiliating experience. I looked at Sandy, "I can't do this anymore. I never want to see her again. I have done everything to love and care for her, but I can no longer be treated this way."

I was trembling and full of rage. I had hit my boiling point. The social worker, my friend, came out of the room and I could see the empathy and compassion in her eyes.

Sandy said, "I will respect whatever you need to do. I understand. But do you think you will be okay with this decision once she dies?"

At that moment, I didn't care. I could not see past that moment. I just knew I needed to cut all ties before it killed me. I left her, my peers, and returned home to sob in my husband's arms.

The man that had been treated so badly by my mother was the one to encouraged me to forgive her and stay the course. He knew the emotional pain I would suffer if I chose differently. If she only knew how much he truly loved me and what a wonderful man I married. That night was a sleepless one.

I visited her the next morning, and it was like nothing ever happened. She greeted me with a hug and kiss and was in a joyful mood. I never knew what I would walk into. That was the norm for as long as I could remember. I continued to call daily on my way to work. I would hear the phone ringing, waiting for her to pick up. I am almost ashamed to say I prayed she wouldn't. That she had died peacefully in her sleep and that this torture would be over. I desperately needed to start the healing process and did not feel I could as long as she was still alive.

Closer to death, she stated she knew my morning calls were just obligatory. She knew I didn't really want to talk. She was right. It took every bit of compassion and fortitude to dial that phone every morning. She took every chance to tell me I abandoned her and chose my husband over her. The guilt she inflicted was palpable. Why couldn't she just be happy for me? Why as a mother wasn't she overjoyed that her daughter had someone there that loved her and cared for her? She was dying, and I was going to live on. She just could not see past the displaced abandonment.

A month before she died, me and my husband wanted to get away for a couple days. We decided to go camping in our little camper that was gifted to us as a wedding gift. Sandy encouraged us to go since I was feeling guilty for leaving my mother's care solely up to her. We left but were called shortly thereafter by Sandy stating mom was hallucinating and was quite agitated. Mom said there are cowboys and Indians in her room, and she needed to kill them. We cut our trip short and came home. Her hallucinations increased towards the end. Most conversations were nonsensical, and she had to be watched closely.

In a lucid moment, she looked at me and said, "I will be dead within a week."

She was right.

Eventually she stopped eating and drinking. She looked at Sandy and I and said, "Ta, Ta. Gotta go."

After that, she became unresponsive. She waited to die until Sunday morning. I received a call at 6:00 A.M. from her caregiver stating she thinks she is dead. I jumped out of bed and drove to her home. I crawled onto the bed and knelt beside her lifeless body.

"Mom, no, no."

I held her hand and it was beginning to turn cold. My two sisters were called as well, and they were on the way. I had 10 minutes alone with her before anyone else showed up. I stroked her hair back and closed her gaping mouth. I gently smoothed her favorite lotion on her hands and arms and talked to her lovingly. I wished her love. I wished her peace. I knew her lifelong pain was over, and she finally felt unconditional love and peace.

The next days were filled with pain and grief. Life felt surreal, just floating through the motions and doing the next needed task with minimal thought. Sandy, Louise, and I gathered around a small table in the eerily silent funeral home mom picked out waiting on the funeral director. The silence was palpable as we fidgeted in our seats.

Months ago, Mom had asked me to go with her to the funeral home of her choosing to make her final arrangements. As much as I did not want to, I agreed. I held her hand as she picked out the box to be cremated in, the urn her ashes would be place in and the gazillion pages of documents that needed to be signed and witnessed. The discomfort of being a part of your parent's cremation and final wishes is gut wrenching.

The funeral director sat down in the waiting chair and shifted uncomfortably. "We have an issue," he said. "The documents your mother signed when she made her arrangements to be cremated were not witnessed at the time of her signing. All children need to now agree to her cremation before we proceed."

I grew increasingly frustrated. "I was there when she signed. Your representative was there, and I saw her sign as witness to the documents."

He said, "The page about cremation was missed. I'm sorry. We need her fourth child to agree."

We practically in unison stated, "We don't know where he is. We won't be able to reach him!"

The funeral director again said we had no choice; the signature was required.

Sandy, over the years has had sporadic communication with our brother who lived somewhere on the other side of the country. She made contact and the documents were eventually signed. Weeks passed as we waited for the cremation to take place. The thought of her laying in a freezing cooler for all that time kept me awake at night.

The funeral service was held at a church mom attended for the last couple years of her life. She became very enmeshed with the church and its numerous members. Her friends were strong advocates of promoting mom's book after she gave them all free copies. Mom secretly confided in me that she gave them out begrudgingly as those cheapskates should have paid for them. The members that attended the services looked at Sandy, Louise, and me with such distain. Why wouldn't they after what was written in her books? The hateful things that mom filled their heads with after church services about her ungrateful, selfish brats that never truly loved her.

I wanted to scream to the rafters that it was all lies. That we loved her, we stayed by her side, we cared for her at home until death, and I held her hand through divorces, depression, her diagnosis, chemo treatments, funeral planning, etc. All of this despite the abuse, the beatings, the lies, the manipulation, and the total dismantling of my soul over the course of my 44 years on this earth. But I didn't. I remained silent and swallowed it down as I stood before her friends as the pastor's sermon echoed words of eternal love and peace.

I returned to work a week later and fell right back into the groove of the intense demands of my position as Director at hospice. I oversaw numerous departments and was responsible for my employees, mentoring, and providing clinical supervision to all therapists and Chaplains. I served on numerous committees and was responsible for budgeting, risk assessments, compliance measures, creation of policies and procedures and growing our bereavement department. I poured myself into my job, my kids, and my husband while working with Sandy in emptying mom's home before it was to be put on the housing market.

It is a widely accepted fact among those in the hospice community that many people experience significant emotional struggles about three months after the death of a loved one. I was no different. The phenomenon is related to the slow down people feel around the three-month mark. The funeral is over, the possessions split up, friends and family members move on with their lives and are not as present to attending your grief, the task-oriented items are wrapping up. Now, it's time for the emotion to really seep in, and the thoughts of grief to take over.

Sandy took on the task of going through all of mom's paperwork. After she completed this monumental task, she handed me a manila folder labeled, *'The true and ugly truth'* with papers in it. "I didn't know if I should give this to you or not, as there are very hurtful things in there, but I decided it's not my choice to make. I took the folder home and held it tightly in my hand. I set it down. I picked it up. I set it down. Is this what she was referring to when I overheard her talking with the aide during her shower?

I picked it up and opened the folder. And it was typewritten letters of her disappointments in me, her disappointment in my decision to marry, her disappointment in my betrayal of her the letters included her memories of childhood, her unrelenting desire to marry, have children, and have those children love and care for her dreams were shattered when she had four children that never really loved her advertisements for attorneys spilled out of the folder and on to the table. She wrote notes on the advertisements that she was coming for me and Tom. I stuffed them back in the folder and closed it shut.

My hands were trembling as I placed the folder on the table. It was as if I could hear her laughing from beyond the grave. "Gotcha."

Amongst her belongings, Sandy found a letter written to her four children asking for us to gather in bright-colored kayaks and spread her ashes in nature, and that is what we did.

A few weeks after her death, I was awoken from such a vivid dream of her that it took minutes to get my bearings. In my dream, she was 25 years old in a long dress with a full-length apron that covered the front and tied at the waist. She looked like she had just stepped off the set of the Little House on the Prairie. Her hair was pulled back in a bun with a handkerchief wrapped around her head and tied in the back. She was laser focused on sweeping the floor with an old straw broom in her hands. I spoke with her fervently firing questions at her.

"What are you doing? Do you like it in heaven? Is this heaven? What is God like?"

She kept methodically sweeping the dusty floor responding to my questions and monotone speech as her eyes never lifted from the floor.

"Annie, there are 11 stages to heaven. I am at level 7. I must earn my way up to the next level. This is my job and I do it all day long."

I woke up and was confused and frustrated. I thought I must go back to sleep and find out more, I needed to know more. What did she mean 'earn her way'? I laid there for what seemed like forever forcing myself to fall back asleep, but slumber never found me. I would have to find peace with what information I had.

As this point, I experienced my first panic attack. I had no idea what was happening to me at the moment. My heart was racing, shaking from head to toe, dizzy, tunnel vision, chest tightness, tachycardia, and cold extremities. I thought I was dying. Heart attack? My husband rushed me to the hospital where numerous tests were done, and I received medicine to calm my heart rate. The doctor was unsure what was wrong, and I was back home. Weeks later, another episode, same outcome. Weeks later, another episode while I was work and a coworker drove me to the hospital. I begged the doctor to tell me what was happening, but again, they did not know. Each time, I was discharged with a different benzodiazepine medication to 'calm my nerves'. I would take one and it would knock me out for up to 24 hours at a time. I hated the effects and would stop after a pill or two.

On the fifth occurrence to the emergency room, the doctor decided to admit me for thorough testing. Five days later and having every test done under the sun, a doctor came in and said, "All this is mental health related. Here is a referral to a psychiatrist for medication and psychologist for therapy."

Mental health issues? How can mental health issues cause such physical symptoms?

"This is ridiculous," I said. "There is something wrong with me!"

There sure was. I was suffering from panic attacks and severe burnout. My nervous system was taxed to the point of absolute exhaustion, and grief was at the heart of it. Grief for the wonderful parts of my mother. Grief for what I never had and never will have. Grief for being an orphan. Grief for my sense of competency, worth and value. Who was I? Where did I go from here?

I took a short leave from work and diligently went to therapy appointments, read self-help books, meditated, did self-hypnosis, exercise, and rested. My therapist taught me about burnout and panic attacks, and how to better manage my stress levels. My panic attacks continued, but now I knew what they were and slowly began to accept them. The key to recovery is not about having anxiety and panic, it's about changing your reaction to it. Befriending it, welcoming it, sitting down at the table beside it and finding gratitude. Sounds strange, doesn't it? The more we fight something, the greater it becomes. Learning to accept something does not mean we like it or want it to continue, it means we stop pushing against it. It's amazing how quickly panic dissipates once you stop fighting.

I eventually went back to work and was thrown right back into my position. My position that dealt with grief, bereavement, and loss. Most peers and employees either avoided or ignored me. They did not know what to do in my presence. Ask if I am recovered from my mental breakdown? Ask what happened? Ask how I am feeling? Avoidance was the choice of many, and for those that stepped up to cover my absence, now stepped back down and animosity set in. Strange how therapists that deal with grief and loss were at a loss as to how to talk to me. Days later, I had my most intense panic attack to date and decided this was no longer the career path I wanted. I picked up my purse, gathered a few belongings and said goodbye to my boss.

Three years before this, I was approached by our medical director asking if I would be interested in going back to school, on the company's dime to get my master's in public or business administration. The CEO was looking to retire soon and was told I would be an excellent fit if I had an education in business. After discussing this with my husband and kids, I graciously accepted and enrolled in classes at our local university for my master's in public administration. It was a huge commitment with three kids at home and working full time, but I was fully committed and had the help and support from my wonderful husband.

After driving away from my last day at hospice, I cried tears of joy and sorrow. I thought for certain this was my career path until retirement. It was my passion, and I was good at it. I had obtained a level I never thought I would reach in my career and now I had no idea what I was going to do now. I was 80 percent finished with my degree at this point, with a 4.0 grade point average. Should I continue? Can I do this? What if I will never be able to work again with these panic attacks? I felt my life was quickly spiraling out of control and the self-doubt set deeply into my soul.

I took a month off to continue working on my recovery before I started looking for work again. I became more comfortable with managing my panic and anxiety. I felt ready to work, I needed to for my self-confidence. I became aware of a leadership position within a prestigious continuous care retirement community and after seven interviews with a trip to the corporate office in Chicago, I was offered the position. I was over the moon and so excited with this new opportunity. It was extremely challenging for the first six months. I was responsible for all 300+ residents, a multi-million-dollar budget and managing numerous employees. I found myself drifting more away from clinical work, and more into the business realm of being part of managing a large community. I grew more and more dissatisfied as most of my day was taken up by meetings and strategic planning. I missed helping people. I missed the intimacy of sitting alongside of a sorrowful patient as they shared their hurts and disappointments.

Alex and Andrew eventually moved in full time with their father when they each turned 18 years old. This was so incredibly difficult for me, because I felt like I was losing them all over again. I felt abandoned and the grief was excruciating. Despite this, I understood completely why the choice was made and loved them just the same. Tom and I had very clear boundaries and expectations of them and now that they were adults, they would need to be responsible for their own finances and needs. With Max, no expectations or boundaries were in place. I knew if I was 18 and, in their shoes, I probably would have made the same decision.

After years of advocating for William and many doctors telling me they did not know why William was the way he was, I found a psychologist that specialized in attention deficit disorder and Autism. William was previously kicked out of several special needs summer camps for angry outbursts and running off. Teachers labeled him with Defiance Disorder and became easily agitated with him.

Within minutes of entering his new psychologist's office, he said "Why hasn't anyone ever previously diagnosed him with autism? It is incredibly obvious." I broke down in tears. Not because of the diagnosis, but finally someone that was able to correctly diagnose my son. Many doors opened for him after his diagnosis. He was eligible for extra services through school, Medicaid and disability. I had to work extremely hard at not blaming myself, as a therapist, for not seeing this earlier. The school system failed him. The doctors failed him. I felt *I* failed him.

Around this time, William had a change in his medication that managed his attention deficit disorder since he was having a difficult time maintaining focus. William's new medication now looked nearly identical to my medication. Mornings were hectic, as I often had employee phone calls before entering the office.

One morning while on a call and trying to juggle meal prep for lunch and making a breakfast smoothie, I accidently took William's medication instead of mine. I realized this right away and the panic welled up inside me. 'It's a stimulant, I thought to myself. What if it triggers panic attacks while I am at work?' I forced myself to put the thought aside and move forward with my day.

I shared my medication mix-up with a trusted peer that morning, and she knew I feared my panic returning.

"No worries. You got this," she said.

"Yes, I got this!"

Later that day my employee, the head of security, and I were in a resident's home because she was trying to get her cat into a cat carrier to take him to the vet. She was frazzled she could not do it. I offered to help and was bitten by the cat. The security officer said he needed to report this incident and I needed to go to the hospital for treatment. I absolutely did not want to go to the hospital since I knew it would bring back bad memories of the previous year.

Policy dictated I must go, so I did. I was treated and per protocol, drug tested as any incident that led to an injury requires a mandatory drug test. I thought nothing of it and went back to work later that day. That evening, I received a phone call asking why I tested positive for amphetamines. Amphetamines? Why would I test positive for that? It suddenly dawned on me that taking William's medication by accident was the reason. I explained this and was called an hour later to be told my employment was terminated immediately due to a positive drug test. I dropped the phone and fell to my knees. This could not be happening. My husband was working out of state for a short period of time and flew home immediately once I called him because I was hysterical. I tried feverishly to explain what happened to my corporate office in an effort to obtain my job back, but to no avail.

The shock, despair and humiliation felt insurmountable. I left my last job in humiliation due to mental health issues, and now for a positive drug test. How would I recover from this? I was angry at God. I screamed at Him to tell me why He continued to lead me to opportunities to have them just ripped away in such a humiliating fashion.

After a few days of tears and self-exploration, I accepted this wasn't my path and He was leading me to do something different.

"God, just show me what you want me to do. Please, I am listening."

The next morning, I woke up with total absolution of my next move. Private practice. I will start my own private practice as this was my goal before entering college. I had complete clarity God closed one door to open the one I am meant to enter. I sat down at my computer and searched, 'How to start your own mental health practice'.

Within three months, I created a business plan, obtained my business license, became paneled with insurance companies, learned about marketing, met with local physicians and therapists, found, and furnished an office space, and started my practice. I was told by a fellow therapist to give it three solid years to get comfortable with running a practice and to have a full caseload. I was determined to accomplish that in one year.

Within eight months, my practice was full, and I was working five jam packed days a week. Those first few months, I focused all profits back into marketing, networking and further education. I became a Certified Hypnotist, Anger Management Specialist, Certified Autism Spectrum Disorder Clinical Specialist, Certified Complex Trauma Professional, and Certified Dementia Care Specialist.

I continued this reinvestment plan monthly, over and over until I was full. My faith steadily grew since the decision to start my practice, and I gave all credit for success to God. He led me and I followed. Simple as that. I started every day with prayer and gratitude and asked for His will be done, not mine. Every new client I obtained; my gratitude went to Him for leading them to me. For every check I received, I thanked Him for His bounty. I thanked Him for closing that door which at the time felt like the end of my career, but really was beginning my new calling.

Chapter Fifteen

"Everything is hard before it is easy."

~ ***Goethe***

Years later, during the onset of COVID, I was going through unopened boxes that were packed up after my mother had died and we were clearing out her home in an effort to sell it. In one of the boxes, I found 3 old cameras my mother had used over the years. All of them required film which at that point was so outdated and difficult to find. I enlisted the help from a friend that was a photographer to guide me on a good starter camera. He got me set up with a Panasonic Lumix bridge camera and gave me photography lessons. My love for photography quickly took off. I spent most of mornings biking to the beach or a park with my camera in tow to capture the wonders of nature. Hundreds upon hundreds of my first photos came out blurry, composition was off, lighting was off, et cetera. I was totally committed to stick with it and to learn the skills needed to hone my skill that quickly became my passion.

In 2022, I began to struggle with mood fluctuations, insomnia, nausea, anxiety, panic attacks, and dizziness. I was terrified that I was having panic attacks again and thought I had a good grip on that because it had been quite some time since my last bout. It took me months before going to the doctor as I had developed a fear of all doctors after all previous medical mishaps I had experienced. By the time I had my appointment, my symptoms dissipated and were mostly gone. He told me I was entering menopause, and that it was normal to feel this way. He expressed it could be months before I felt symptoms again, and he was right.

Almost a year passed, and the symptoms returned with a vengeance. For weeks, I only slept a couple of hours a night, I was so dizzy daily, I thought I was going to pass out, nausea, anxiety, and constant panic attacks. As soon as one ended, another hit. I decided I would read everything I could get my hands on to educate myself about hormones and menopause. I read books, listened to podcasts, joined a menopause support group, had a virtual consult with a famous OBGYN in France, did blood work and hormone testing, frequented my nutritionist's office and took supplements, herbs, etc. After all my research, I decided hormone replacement therapy was the next best step for me.

I went back to the doctor, and he prescribed estrogen, and I happily took it. I felt great for the first week, and then hit a wall. Over the next few months, I became increasingly worse, and my symptoms then became debilitating. I was so exhausted, and my nervous system was so frayed that I decided to take a month off work and recover. My body made the decision for me because I could no longer function. This produced such guilt and shame within me as I felt I was abandoning and letting my clients down.

Some really needed me, and I just could not be there for them. I could barely get out of bed. I fell into depression like no other time before. This eventually gave way to having thoughts of ending my life as I could no longer stand the suffering. The thoughts persisted until I began formulating a plan. I knew this was the moment I needed to reach out to a therapist but did not have the mental fortitude to do so. I hid this from my husband because I did not want to appear weak. Us therapists are supposed to have it all figured out, right? I mentally began to divide up my possessions as to who would get what. I began to write my wishes down in a notebook and mentally formulated how to say goodbye to my husband and children. I cried as I stared at the next blank page while my thoughts drifted to my husband and children. I closed the notebook and crawled back into bed.

I reluctantly linked with a therapist, and I scheduled one last appointment with my nutritionist. She did the lab work for my hormone levels and had to wait two weeks for the results. In the meantime, I connected with a private menopause group on Facebook. I poured out my heart and soul to the group, and someone responded, 'I think you have too much estrogen and need to stop. You also need progesterone'. I started researching progesterone and how estrogen should never be taken without Progesterone. Estrogen is the lion and Progesterone is the lion tamer.

I called my OBGYN and ask for progesterone, but he said, "No, I don't do that. Go to a specialist."

A specialist? Aren't OBGYNs supposed to know about menopause and hormones? Aren't they the specialists? All the referred 'specialists' were booked out for months, so I took things into my own hands.

On a wing and a prayer, I stopped estrogen, bought progesterone over the counter and practically bathed in it to help even out my hormones. My hormone test results finally came back in, and my nutritionist called me and left a message to call her immediately. I did so and she stated, "Stop the estrogen now! The normal range is .9 to 1.9 and yours is 69. I can't believe you're even functioning at this point. No wonder you're feeling the way you do." I explained that I decided on my own to stop estrogen and put myself on progesterone; she agreed. I hung up the phone and cried. The pieces of the puzzle were finally coming together. Over the next couple weeks, my symptoms subsided, and I was able to crawl out of the hole I was so deeply in and get back to work. I give full credit to the strong women in that Facebook support group for guiding and educating me about estrogen dominance and the need for progesterone, and to my husband for his unwavering love and support.

I have now heard from hundreds of women who have had similar experiences as I have. The unrelenting pain and suffering I have heard from these women was mind boggling. Why was this so prevalent in the year 2024?

Why were doctors writing prescription after prescription for hormone treatments but not prescribing based off the presenting symptoms of estrogen dominant women? I decided to take the education I obtained, my experience, and apply it towards helping other woman suffering from perimenopause and menopause. No woman should have to suffer in silence or at the hands of uneducated medical professionals. To further my education in this area, I obtained my certification as an Integrative Mental Health Professional and now specialize in supporting and educating menopausal women.

Epilogue

"It's never too late to be what you might've been."

~ ***George Eliot***

Since then, I have been working with a therapist every week doing Eye Movement Desensitization and Reprocessing (EMDR) therapy to heal my fear of doctors and hospitals and address issues related to Complex Post Traumatic Stress Disorder (C-PTSD). I am a firm believer in the power and healing of therapy in the hands of a skilled therapist. Therapists need therapists. We are human just like everyone else. I tell my clients who are embarrassed about going to therapy, "You are the strong and courageous one. Therapy is sometimes painful, dirty work that can create discomfort and pain as we sift through the traumatic memories, disappointments, shame, and guilt. It's easier to bury things away than addressing them. You chose not to do that. Your reward will be the healing of your wounds and the change in your behavior." I must remind myself of this as well.

One of my dreams was to someday combine wildlife photography and biblical verses into a book. Eventually, I felt my photography was at a level I could start making this dream come true. I read all I could on publishing, self-publishing, printing, editing, marketing, and copywriting. I started my own photography business while lying in bed for two weeks recovering from COVID. After hours and hours of hair pulling and trial and error, I completed and published my wildlife book coupled with biblical verses.

I recently applied and was accepted into a doctorate program at the University of Kentucky. People often ask me what I will do with the doctorate. Teach? Increase my rates? I say neither. I love to learn, and I want to be the very best I can to be of service and heal my clients. And with full disclosure, part of me wants to prove to myself that I can. At 52 years old, who knows where life will lead me next. I have also recently completed training to be a EMDR therapist so I can help others heal from trauma.

Some days I sit and look over my years on earth and think about the pain, joyous moments, the disappointments, and accomplishments, the love I have given and received, and the grace I have been given and hopefully gave. I wouldn't change a moment for anything. It has all lead me to where I am now. Three beautiful adult children that are healthy, happy and the biggest and best accomplishment of my life. A loving, healthy relationship with a man that is my anchor in any storm. A man that was and is a good father figure and role model for our children. A career, two businesses, my education, and accomplishments that I was told I could and would never achieve.

I caught myself once looking to heaven and asking, "Who's having the last laugh now? You said I could never do it, but I did." But as quickly as the thought came, I shifted my thinking to gratitude and grace. I forgive her for her inability to heal her own wounds. I forgive her for continuing the pattern of generational abuse. I forgive her for breaking my spirit and having to rebuild my confidence and my self-image. I acknowledge that she did the best she could with what she had. I acknowledge that she loved me and fiercely protected me when in danger. I acknowledge the pattern of abuse stopped with me. I acknowledge I am strong. I am resilient. I am enough.

Through the Grace of God go I. If I can do it, so can you.

Resources

- National Suicide Hotline- 1-800-273-TALK(8255) Beginning 7/16/2022 dial 988 for Suicide Hotline
- For TTY users: Use your preferred relay service or dial 711 then 988 www.988LIFELINE.ORG
- Alcohol Resource Center 1-800-839-1686
- Substance Abuse and Mental Health Services Administration (SAMHSA) 1-800-662-HELP (4357). www.samhsa.org
- Adult Children of Alcoholics & Dysfunctional Families: 1-310-534-1815
- National Association for Children of Alcoholics 1-888-554-2627 National Domestic Violence Hotline: 1-800-799-7233. Text START to 88788
- Postpartum Support International: 1-800-944-4773 Post Abortion Hotline: 1-800-228-0332
- Crisis Pregnancy Hotline: 1-800-67-BABY-6 Child Help Hotline: 1-800-422-4453
- Child Welfare Information Gateway: 1-800-394-3366 Child Abuse National Hotline: 1-800-25ABUSE National Sexual Assault Hotline: 1-800-656-4673 Grief/Loss GriefShare: 1800-395-5755
- Youth Crisis Hotline: 1-800-448-4663

www.ingramcontent.com/pod-product-compliance
Lightning Source LLC
LaVergne TN
LVHW022215200926
848481LV00006B/1977